UNEP
YEAR
BOOK

EMERGING ISSUES
IN OUR GLOBAL ENVIRONMENT

2011

UNEP

United Nations Environm

Table of Contents

Preface

The world is again on the Road to Rio, almost 20 years after the Earth Summit of 1992 that laid out the treaties, policies and principles towards sustainable development.

The intervening years have witnessed an extraordinary explosion in scientific understanding of the impacts of human activity on the planet and atmosphere.

That science has informed policymakers on the options and choices for change and has assisted in evolving responses, such as the greenhouse gas emission reduction treaty—the Kyoto Protocol—or more recently a decision to establish an International Regime on Access and Benefit Sharing of Genetic Resources at the Convention on Biological Diversity (CBD) meeting in Nagoya, Japan last year.

The UNEP Year Book 2011 underlines some of the successes achieved when science is fully brought into service for sustainable development. Yet, it also spotlights that many of the international responses to the challenges remain at best a patchwork: at worst, often far behind the scale and pace of environmental change being witnessed today.

The 2011 Year Book showcases and explains three emerging issues. The first—the wider impacts of phosphorus use in food production, pointing to concerns over the future availability of phosphorus supplies —in contrast with the millions of tonnes of fertilizer washed from the land into the seas triggering algal blooms and damage to fish stocks and tourism-based industries.

It also spotlights growing scientific concern over the chemical and material impact of marine litter on wildlife and the human food chain, as well as the crucial role of biodiversity in maintaining healthy forests.

With the right public policies and enabling conditions, these challenges can be addressed in ways that reduce humanity's environmental footprint while generating new kinds of business and employment, for example in sustainable waste management—one of the ten sectors identified as key to catalysing a transition to a low carbon, resource efficient Green Economy.

The window for action is narrowing. As the Year Book underlines, persistent issues are in many cases becoming more acute, whilst new ones are emerging.

Next year at Rio+20, governments need to urgently address the gap between science and how to form a decisive response as part of an overall package that finally aligns the economic pillar of sustainable development with the social and environmental ones.

The UNEP Year Book 2011 is a snapshot of the world 15 months before Rio+20—perhaps future Year Books may reflect a different story as a result of the evolutionary decisions taken in Brazil in 2012.

Achim Steiner

United Nations Under-Secretary-General and Executive Director, United Nations Environment Programme

Executive Summary

The UNEP Year Book series provides an annual update on new science and developments. It brings emerging environmental issues to the attention of governments and other stakeholders for their consideration. The Year Book is part of a suite of UNEP products whose aim is to strengthen the science-to-policy interface.

The events and developments presented in the UNEP Year Book 2011 remind us that it is urgent to achieve results in the international climate change processes. Although countries' greenhouse gas reduction pledges are contributing significantly to the emission reductions required to keep the temperature increase during the 21st century below 2°C, scientists warn that there is still a considerable 'emission gap' of 5 gigatonnes to be closed. The need to reduce emissions of black carbon and tropospheric ozone precursors has received comparatively little attention so far. New science shows that reducing such air pollutants could go a long way towards mitigating climate change in the short term, while also improving human health and food security.

A global dialogue on greening the economy has begun, driven by environmental concerns and economic opportunities. While countries have renewed their commitments to work towards environmental sustainability, and have agreed on global strategies for doing so, the private sector is responding to new business opportunities and signals that threats to ecosystems could undermine their operations. The rapid expansion of mobile technology is creating new possibilities to further engage citizens in environmental decision making. Citizen science can help to address important data gaps, especially with respect to biodiversity monitoring.

Today the human footprint extends to the remotest parts of the ocean. Even there, plastic can be found. The ocean has become a global repository for much of the waste we generate. Every year large amounts of plastic debris enter the marine environment, where it slowly fragments and accumulates in convergence zones. In particular, scientists are looking at the potential impacts of small plastic fragments, or microplastics. The role of plastics as a vector for transporting chemicals and species in the ocean is as yet poorly understood, but it poses a potential threat to ecosystems and human health. A number of scientists are concerned about releases of persistent, bio-accumulating and toxic compounds when plastic debris enters the food chain through ingestion by fish and other marine organisms.

Plastic debris can damage nets, foul propellers, and pollute beaches and other areas, with major economic impacts on the fishing and tourist industries. Local governments and other bodies spend millions of dollars per year on cleaning up plastic and other marine litter. To reduce the volume of plastic entering the ocean, all aspects of waste management need to be improved and existing policy instruments strengthened.

Phosphorus is a critical nutrient for food production. Further insight is needed into the long-term availability of this essential plant nutrient and the environmental consequences of its use. Agricultural practices commonly include the application of phosphorus fertilizers made from phosphate rock, a non-renewable resource used increasingly since the late 19th century. While several countries have commercially exploitable amounts of phosphate rock, those countries with no domestic reserves could be especially vulnerable to global shortfalls.

Over four times as much phosphorus flows through the environment today as before phosphorus fertilizer began to be used in agriculture, yet only small amounts are recovered and recycled from waste streams. Optimization of agricultural practices, erosion control and the exploration of innovative approaches, such as phosphorus recovery from water treatment installations, would reduce environmental pressures and enhance long-term phosphorus supply.

Our knowledge and understanding of biodiversity have never been greater than they are today. But neither have the pressures on biodiversity ever been greater. Loss of forest biodiversity can reduce the resilience of forests and leave them increasingly vulnerable to mounting pressures, as shown in the example of the mountain pine beetle outbreak presented in the Year Book. Strongly focusing on forests as the key to managing the world's carbon stocks—while disregarding the important role of biodiversity in building forest resilience—may lead to major investments in systems that are vulnerable to fire or pest outbreaks, which could nullify gains made in carbon sequestration.

Conservation of forest biodiversity is fundamental to sustaining forests and people in a world that is adapting to climate change. Ecosystem-based approaches recognize the importance of biodiversity and the need for broad stakeholder participation in forest-related decision making in order to arrive at more effective conservation outcomes. New approaches to biodiversity conservation are promising, but they need to be matched by more effective governance and greater financial investments.

Environmental indicators such as those in the Year Book can help assess the impacts of complex interactions between people and the environment. The latest available data and trends show progress in addressing stratospheric ozone depletion, the need for more renewable energy and the need for environmental certification schemes. Global carbon dioxide emissions are still increasing and pressures on ecosystems from the use of natural resources continue, with notable impacts in terms of biodiversity loss. Poor availability of environmental data—especially from developing countries—remains a major constraint on identifying and following global environmental trends.

The Year Book gives numerous examples of practical measures that can be taken to prevent further pollution and resource depletion. However, the persistence of environmental problems tracked over time also shows that there is still much room to improve the effectiveness of environmental governance.

As countries prepare for the World Summit in 2012 in Brazil (Rio+20), it is important to signal emerging challenges that could undermine sustainable development efforts - alongside promising signs that countries, companies and communities are starting to embrace the transition to a low-carbon, resource-efficient economy.

UNEP welcomes your feedback. Readers are invited to use the questionnaire form available at www.unep.org/yearbook/2011/

Credit: Vera Kratochvil
Credit: Project Kaisei
Credit: D.M.G. de Sousa
Credit: José Badelles
Credit: Edward Obi-Akpere

On 140 acres of unused land at Nellis Air Force Base, Nevada, United States, 70 000 solar panels are part of a solar photovoltaic array that will generate15 megawatts of solar power for the base. *Credit: Nadine Y. Barclay/USAF*

Events and Developments

Driven by environmental concerns and economic opportunities, a global dialogue on greening the economy has begun. Countries have renewed their commitments to work towards environmental sustainability at various international fora, and some have initiated national actions. The private sector is responding not only to clean technology and green investment opportunities, but also to signals that threats to ecosystems could have serious impacts on business operations. At the same time, scientists and others point out multiple approaches and technologies available for the reduction of greenhouse gas emissions. These international events and developments—together with a series of extreme weather events—continue to urge us to achieve results in international climate change processes.

Environmental events and developments during the past year present a mixed picture. A review of the status of the achievement of the Millennium Development Goals (MDGs) in September showed that many countries, including some of the poorest, have made good progress. However, more efforts are required in regard to Goal 7 on ensuring environmental sustainability. Rapid biodiversity loss has not been halted, but in October governments agreed on new targets. They also agreed to establish a new body to provide the science-policy interface for biodiversity. The latest round of climate negotiations, held in December in Cancún, Mexico, put the world's efforts on climate change back on track. The package of decisions agreed succeeded in 'anchoring' the national targets and actions governments had put forward in and after the 2009 climate conference in Copenhagen, Denmark. Nevertheless, a significant emissions gap exists between what is being promised by countries and what is needed to keep the rise in global temperature below 2°C. Agreeing a process to close this gap will be one of the major challenges at the global climate negotiations in 2011 in Durban, South Africa.

2010 was a year of extreme weather. The World Meteorological Organization (WMO) reported that it tied with 1998 and 2005 as the warmest years on record (WMO 2011). There were 950 major natural disasters in 2010 compared to 785 in 2009. The heat wave in the Russian Federation and in particular the flooding in Pakistan resulting from an unusual stagnant jet stream, caused the loss of many lives (Red Cross 2011). Still unclear are the environmental impacts stemming from the months-long discharge of crude oil into the Gulf of Mexico that will go on record as one of history's worst oil spill disasters. The environmental impacts will be monitored over the next few years and are continuously evaluated.

Sustainable development and a green economy

While the world is slowly recovering from economic and financial crises, a global dialogue on natural capital and greening the economy has begun in countries, communities and companies. The need for urgent action to address climate change in the first half of the 21st century is fostering this dialogue, which is also stimulated by abundant potential economic opportunities for those who undertake the transition to a green economy.

A decade after the 2000 Millennium Summit, governments met at the High-level Plenary Meeting of the 65th Session of the UN General Assembly to review progress on achieving the MDGs and to renew their commitment to achieve the targets for 2015. Developing countries have made major progress on the health and education targets, but global progress has been slow on other goals, including ensuring environmental sustainability (IISD 2010, UNGA 2010). Key areas where progress on this goal could be accelerated include:

- implementation of the three UN Conventions on combating desertification, biological diversity and climate change, as well as the global objectives on forests and sustainable forest management;
- new and renewable energy sources, low-emission technologies, more efficient energy use, greater reliance on advanced energy technologies, and sustainable use of traditional energy sources;
- sustainable access to safe drinking water and basic sanitation;
- integrated waste management systems;
- sustainable management of marine biodiversity and ecosystems, and preservation of fragile mountain ecosystems;
- sustainable consumption and production patterns.

Calendar of events 2010

JANUARY
12 January
Magnitude 7.0 earthquake kills some 230 000 people and leaves 1.5 million homeless in the region around Haiti's capital, Port-au-Prince. Cholera outbreak in October claims more than 1 200 lives, as tens of thousands of Haitians are still living in crowded tent cities with poor sanitation and little access to clean drinking water.

FEBRUARY
24-26 February
Eleventh Special Session of UNEP Governing Council/Global Ministerial Environment Forum delivers first landmark Declaration issued by ministers of the environment in a decade, pledging to step up global response to major environmental and sustainability challenges. Governments also agree on co-operative action by the Basel, Rotterdam and Stockholm Conventions.

27 February
Earthquake in central Chile measuring 8.8 kills more than 700 and causes widespread damage in many parts of the country, particularly near Concepción, the second largest metropolitan area. Around half a million homes are seriously damaged. Losses to Chile's economy are estimated at US$15-30 billion.

Credit: Pan-African News Wire File Photos

MARCH
13-25 March
Fifteenth Conference of the Parties to Convention on International Trade in Endangered Species of Wild Fauna and Flora (CITES) adopts decisions on strengthening wildlife management for several reptiles, combating illegal tiger and rhinoceros trafficking, and updating trade rules for a wide range of plants and animals.

18-19 March
Fourth meeting of UN-REDD Programme Policy Board approves US$14.7 million in funding for national climate change mitigation programmes in Bolivia, the Democratic Republic of the Congo and Zambia. US$15.2 million approved in November for programmes in Cambodia, Papua New Guinea, Paraguay, the Philippines and the Solomon Islands.

APRIL
14-20 April
Ash covers large areas of northern Europe when Iceland's Eyjafjallajoekull volcano erupts. About 20 countries close their airspace, affecting hundreds of thousands of travellers worldwide. The grounding of European flights avoided an estimated 344 109 tonnes of CO_2 emissions per day while the volcano emitted about 150 000 tonnes of CO_2 per day.

Credit: Eyjólfur Magnússon

20 April
Oil rig 'Deepwater Horizon' explodes in the Gulf of Mexico, resulting in the largest accidental marine oil spill in the petroleum industry's history and causing damage to wildlife and marine habitats, and to the fishing and tourism industries. Five million barrels flow into the Gulf before the well is permanently sealed on 19 September.

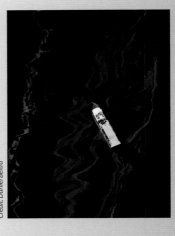
Credit: Daniel Beltrá

MAY
3-14 May
Eighteenth session of United Nations Commission on Sustainable Development (CSD) focuses on the thematic cluster of transport, chemicals, waste management, mining, and sustainable consumption and production patterns. Ways to advance implementation of decisions of the Commission are discussed.

12 May
Abu Dhabi, United Arab Emirates, wins Arab world's top 'green city' and 'most environmentally friendly city' awards. This double recognition is announced at a ceremony for Arab cities leading in environment, greening and landscaping, technology and architecture.

20 May
Scientists develop first living cell controlled by a synthetic genome. They hope this method can be used to engineer bacteria designed to solve environmental or energy problems, for example algae that capture CO_2 and make new hydrocarbons that could be used in refineries.

17-19 May
First session of Preparatory Committee (PrepCom) for 2012 United Nations Conference on Sustainable Development assesses gaps in implementing outcomes of major summits on sustainable development and emerging challenges, and agrees on 'open-ended informal intersessional meetings' of not more than six days in length.

24-28 May
Fourth Global Environment Facility (GEF) Assembly at Punta del Este, Uruguay, agrees on basic financing framework, and a replenishment of US$4.2 billion. Contributing to the GEF Trust Fund is one way for governments to comply with their commitments under multilateral environmental agreements.

JUNE
5 June
World Environment Day celebrations in Rwanda culminate in traditional gorilla-naming ceremony in Volcanoes National Park, attended by 30 000 people. Rwandan President Paul Kagame, actor and UNEP Goodwill Ambassador Don Cheadle, and UNEP Executive Director Achim Steiner are among the guests invited to name baby gorillas.

Credit: www.wildlifedirect.org

20-25 June
Thirteenth session of the African Ministerial Conference on the Environment (AMCEN) in Mali adopts the Bamako Declaration, a new road map for sustainable development in Africa and a basis for strengthening the common negotiating position on climate change and biological diversity.

JULY
July-August
Heaviest monsoon rains in over 80 years produce the worst floods in Pakistan's history, destroying homes and farmland and affecting an estimated 3.2 million people. The number of livestock lost is around 80 000, while 2 million hectares of farmland are underwater.

Credit: Ax Grift

AUGUST
4 August
Giant chunk of ice breaks off Petermann glacier in northwest Greenland, forming the largest iceberg in the northern hemisphere. Measuring about 30 by 14 kilometres, it covers an area of some 245 square kilometres. The Petermann glacier, one of Greenland's largest, regularly advances towards the ocean at about 1 kilometre per year.

Credit: NASA Earth Observatory

1-26 August
Wildfires sweeping across Russia destroy more than 300 000 hectares of forest, vegetation and peatland. At least 53 people are killed and thousands are evacuated. In Bolivia, wildfires ravage 1.5 million hectares of forests and grasslands.

SEPTEMBER
20-22 September
United Nations Summit on the Millennium Development Goals (MDGs) concludes with the adoption of a global action plan to achieve the eight MDGs by their 2015 target. Major new commitments and initiatives are announced, including on ensuring environmental sustainability.

OCTOBER
5 October
In Hungary, toxic red sludge from an alumina plant floods nearby villages. Ten people are killed and 120 injured. Some 600 000 to 700 000 cubic metres of sludge escapes. It is estimated that the clean-up will take more than a year and cost tens of millions of dollars.

Credit: Varga György/MTI Fotó

12-15 October
Seventh African Development Forum convenes with the theme 'Acting on Climate Change for Sustainable Development in Africa'. Among the outcomes is the establishment of a partnership on 'Africa's options for a Green Economy'.

18-29 October
At the Biodiversity Summit in Nagoya, Japan, participants representing the 193 Parties to the Convention on Biological Diversity (CBD) adopt a new ten-year Strategic Plan to guide efforts to save biodiversity and the Nagoya Protocol on Access to Genetic Resources and the Fair and Equitable Sharing of Benefits Arising from their Utilization.

Credit: International Institute for Sustainable Development

26 October
Hunters' reports lead scientists to discover a new primate species, the Myanmar snub-nosed monkey (Rhinopithecus strykeri), in the country's northern forests. Local people report that it is easy to find the monkey, which sneezes when it rains.

NOVEMBER
8-12 November
Twenty-second session of the Meeting of the Parties to the Montreal Protocol on Substances that Deplete the Ozone Layer adopts 16 decisions, including on the terms of reference for evaluating the financial mechanism. It is unable to make progress on low global warming potential alternatives or the destruction of ozone destroying substances.

10-11 November
In Seoul, Republic of Korea, for the first time at a G-20 meeting, more than 100 Chief Executive Officers (CEOs) meet to review strategies for a greener global economy. Corporate leaders from 34 countries urge the G-20 to facilitate green growth, including improvements in energy efficiency and creation of 'green jobs'.

21-23 November
At its second meeting in Helsinki, Finland, the Consultative Group of Ministers or High-level Representatives on International Governance identifies potential system-wide responses to the challenges of international environmental governance. They include strengthening the science-policy interface and developing a system-wide strategy for environment in the United Nations system.

21-24 November
Heads of governments of 13 Tiger Range Countries at the International Tiger Conservation Forum in St Petersburg, Russia, agree to save wild tigers from extinction and double their number by 2022. Worldwide, the population of tigers in the wild fell from 100 000 to just over 3 000 during the past century.

Credit: Valerie Abbott

29 November-10 December
Cancún Climate Change Conference in Mexico sets governments on a path towards a low-emissions future and enhanced action on climate change in the developing world. Parties to the Kyoto Protocol agree to continue negotiations, with the aim of ensuring that there is no gap between its commitment periods.

DECEMBER
3 December
Ten European countries agree to develop an offshore electricity grid in the North Sea costing up to US$40 billion. The ultimate vision is a European 'supergrid' providing renewable energy supplies throughout Europe by tapping into vast solar resources from the Mediterranean and wind from the north.

Credit: UNEP

21 December
United Nations General Assembly adopts the creation of the Intergovernmental Platform on Biodiversity and Ecosystem Services (IPBES) after governments gave a green light in June at a meeting in Busan, Republic of Korea. The body will carry out high-quality peer reviews of new science on biodiversity and ecosystems and outline policy responses.

31 December-January
More than 200 000 people are affected by flooding in Queensland state, northeast Australia, with the flood zone stretching over an area bigger than France and Germany combined. Thousands of people are evacuated from their homes. Cleanup efforts are expected to cost billions of dollars.

Sources: Please go to www.unep.org/yearbook/2011/

Also emphasized at the summit were the need for greater co-ordination among local and national institutions responsible for economic and social development and environmental protection, and the need to encourage investments in sustainable development (UNGA 2010).

The challenge of promoting sustainable development while achieving economic growth is motivating decision makers to take a serious look at policy measures oriented towards green growth and innovation (G20 Seoul Summit 2010). For example, the Republic of Korea spends the equivalent of more than 3 per cent of its annual GDP on green technology (Barbier 2009).

The development and uptake of renewable energy technologies is rapidly gaining momentum, creating millions of jobs. More opportunities to create 'green jobs' are emerging in natural resource management, sustainable food production, waste processing and other fields.

The green economy promises to create more 'green jobs' in the future. *Credit: Sam Hummel*

Renewable energy

Climate change, pollution, resource depletion, and the desire for energy security are persuading countries to make the transition from energy supply based on fossil fuels alone to greater energy efficiency and the use of renewable energy sources—thereby contributing to the transition to a green economy (Brown 2009). While China overtook the United States in 2010 as the world's largest energy user, it has also become a renewable energy leader, especially for wind and solar power (IEA 2010a). Global new investment in sustainable energy reached US$162 billion in 2009, adding an estimated 50 gigawatts (GW) of renewable energy generation capacity in addition to 28 GW of new large hydroelectric capacity. If the trend continues, 2011 could be the first year that new low-carbon energy capacity exceeds new fossil-fuel capacity (UNEP and Bloomberg New Energy Finance 2010). This is supported by other signs of a more permanent shift towards sustainable energy, such as an accelerating energy efficiency improvement rate; growth in public investment in low-carbon technology research, development and demonstration; and further development of hybrid and fully electric vehicles by leading companies (IEA 2010a).

The latest available data show that in 2009, for the second year in a row, both Europe and the United States added more power capacity from renewable sources such as wind and solar than from conventional sources like coal, gas and nuclear. Renewables accounted for 60 per cent of newly installed capacity in Europe and more than 50 per cent of that in the United States in 2009. By 2010 or 2011, experts predict that the world as a whole will add more capacity to the electricity supply from renewable than non-renewable sources (REN 21 2010, UNEP and Bloomberg New Energy Finance 2010). Demand for renewable energy is expected to triple over the next decades, with its share in electricity supply increasing from one-fifth to one-third (**Figure 1**).

To achieve a low-carbon future, increased energy efficiency is essential. Low-cost options for reducing energy consumption in buildings can contribute significantly to cuts in CO_2 emissions (**Box 1**). Around 10 per cent of global CO_2 emissions come directly from buildings; when indirect emissions from their electricity use are included, this share increases to almost 30 per cent (IEA 2010a).

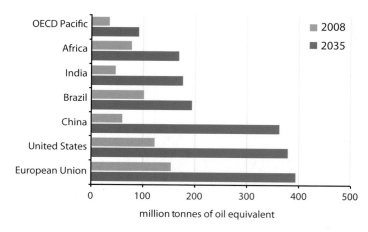

Figure 1: Projected renewable energy demand, 2008-2035. The share of renewables in global electricity generation is projected to increase from 19 to 32 per cent between 2008 and 2035, mainly due to increases in wind and hydropower. *Source: IEA (2010b)*

Leading by example within the United Nations System: UNEP and UN-Habitat move to energy-efficient offices in Nairobi, Kenya. *Credit: Márton Bálint*

Box 1: Energy saving in buildings

Many consumers in the future may have smart meters in their homes to track and manage energy use, although practical applications of this technology are still being assessed. About 20 per cent of the energy used in buildings could potentially be saved through correcting mechanical faults and malfunctions and reducing unnecessary operation. Initial deployments of advanced control systems currently under development suggest that such systems could save an additional 10 to 20 per cent. It is possible to reduce real-time energy use and save energy by allowing electricity providers to manage loads, for example through the use of internet-based intelligent infrastructure that works with a 'smart grid' to switch off air conditioning equipment during peak demand periods. In the United States, buildings use 40 per cent of all primary energy supplied (and more than 70 per cent of all electricity generated), predominantly for heating, cooling and lighting (Gershenfeld and others 2010).

Keeping the climate momentum going

At the end of 2010, governments reaffirmed their commitment to combat climate change at the UN Climate Change Conference in Cancún, Mexico. They agreed to a process to design a Green Climate Fund; a new Adaptation Framework to allow better planning and implementation of adaptation projects; and a technology mechanism with a Technology Executive Committee and Climate Technology Centre and Network to increase technology co-operation in support of action on adaptation and mitigation. They also agreed to boost action to curb emissions from deforestation and forest degradation in developing countries with technological and financial support, and reaffirmed the goal set in Copenhagen in 2009 to provide US$100 billion annually in aid for poor countries up to 2020 (UNEP 2010a).

Alongside the formal discussions in Cancún, a series of events brought together heads of state and representatives of regional and local governments, business and civil society, showcasing how some sectors, communities and individuals are rapidly moving ahead to make the transition to a low-carbon future. National strategies are being developed in many countries, including Mexico and Uruguay. This momentum is essential to the campaign to combat climate change.

In the lead-up to Cancún, UNEP and climate scientists published a report showing that a significant emissions gap exists between what is being promised by countries and what is needed to keep a global temperature rise below 2°C in the twenty-first century. That gap remains post Cancún. The report estimated that, to have a likely chance of staying below 2°C, global emissions need to peak at around 44 gigatonnes (Gt) of CO_2 equivalent in 2020. Fully implementing the pledges and intentions associated with the Copenhagen Accord and now reflected in the Cancún Agreements (**Figure 2**), could in the best case identified by the report, cut emissions to around 49 Gt of CO_2 equivalent by 2020. This would leave a gap of around 5 Gt of CO_2 equivalent that needs to be bridged over the coming decade—an amount equal to the emissions of all the world's cars, buses and trucks in 2005 (UNEP 2010b).

Investments of more than US$2 trillion per year in infrastructure alone between 2010 and 2030 are necessary to achieve the 2°C goal. The UNFCCC Secretariat has estimated that 86 per cent of the funding required for investments in developing countries will come from the private sector (UNFCCC 2007). Companies are willing to consider this type of investment if it makes strategic business sense in the long term and offers adequate risk-adjusted financial returns (WBCSD 2010). A recent analysis of major international companies supports this

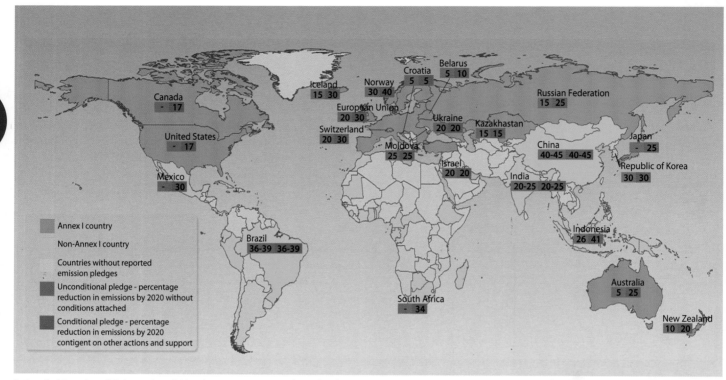

Figure 2: More than 22 Annex I and Non-Annex I countries (industrialized and developing countries, respectively), together with the European Union, have pledged to reduce their greenhouse gas (GHG) emissions, in CO_2 equivalent, by 2020. The map shows the status as of 31 December 2010. Not shown are Costa Rica (which expects to become carbon neutral by 2021) and Papua New Guinea (which plans to decrease its GHG emissions by at least 50 per cent before 2030 and become carbon neutral before 2050). *Source: UNEP (2010b)*

assessment, showing that companies that lead in climate-related innovation also have higher economic performance. Innovation and development of new technologies, marketing strategies and partnerships position these companies to seize opportunities and achieve sustained growth in a carbon-constrained future business environment (Maplecroft 2010a).

The scientific focus has recently been shifting towards measures to avoid dangerous warming by reducing emissions other than those of carbon dioxide. Reduced emissions of air pollutants such as black carbon, tropospheric ozone and ozone precursors, including methane, not only help to mitigate climate change, but also benefit human health by improving air quality (**Box 2**). As most substances that deplete the stratospheric ozone layer are also greenhouse gases, regulation under the Montreal Protocol has already prevented 135 Gt of CO_2 equivalent in greenhouse gas emissions over the past two decades (Velders et al. 2007). However, hydrochlorofluorocarbons (HCFCs) and their replacement hydrofluorocarbons (HFCs) are both greenhouse gases and the ultimate significance of the climate benefits will depend on which replacement technologies are adopted by countries. Further phase down of HFCs, accelerated phasing out of HCFCs, and the recovery and destruction of ozone depleting substances in waste products are additional regulatory strategies that could be implemented in the near term (Molina et al. 2010). Recent work by scientists and other experts are drawing attention to climate change mitigation opportunities emerging from reducing non-carbon dioxide greenhouse gases, such as black carbon and tropospheric ozone.

Box 2: Reducing black carbon and tropospheric ozone

Aerosols are collections of airborne solid or liquid particles (other than pure water) that reside in the atmosphere for at least several hours. They may be natural or anthropogenic in origin.

Black carbon refers to black carbon-containing aerosols formed through incomplete combustion of fossil fuels, biofuels and biomass. Primary sources include emissions from diesel engines, cooking stoves and forest fires. Although black carbon remains in the atmosphere for only days to weeks, it has recently emerged as an important contributor to climate change.

Methane (CH_4) is a greenhouse gas more than 25 times as effective in trapping heat in the atmosphere as carbon dioxide (CO_2) over a 100-year period. It is emitted from both natural and human-influenced sources. The latter include landfills, natural gas and petroleum systems, agricultural activities, coal mining, wastewater treatment and certain industrial processes. Methane is also a tropospheric ozone precursor.

Ozone (O_3) is a gaseous atmospheric constituent. In the troposphere, the lowest part of the atmosphere (within 8-15 km of the Earth's surface) where clouds and weather phenomena occur, ozone is created by photochemical reactions involving gases that result from both natural and human activities. In high concentrations, tropospheric ozone can be harmful to a wide range of living organisms. It also acts as a greenhouse gas. Ozone in the stratosphere protects against ultraviolet (UV) radiation.

Ozone precursors are chemical compounds which, in the presence of solar radiation, react with other chemical compounds to form ozone in the troposphere.

Particulate matter consists of very small pieces of solid or liquid matter such as particles of soot (black carbon), dust, fumes, mists or aerosols.

Radiative forcing is a measure of how the energy balance of the Earth-atmosphere system with space is influenced when factors that affect the climate are altered. The influence of a factor that can cause climate change, such as a greenhouse gas, is often evaluated in terms of its radiative forcing. The word 'radiative' arises because these factors change the balance between incoming solar radiation and outgoing infrared radiation within the Earth's atmosphere. This radiative balance controls the Earth's surface temperature.

Source: Adapted from IPCC (2007) and US EPA (2011)

Limiting climate change and improving air quality are two of the most pressing environmental challenges. They are also closely linked. There is a broad consensus that action is required to address near-term climate change in the first half of this century, as well as to protect the climate in the long-term. Efforts to reduce CO_2 emissions in order to protect the long-term climate need to start now, even though they will not significantly affect near-term climate change. However, these efforts will be most effective if emissions of the 'short-lived climate forcers' (SLCFs) are reduced, especially those of black carbon, tropospheric ozone, and the tropospheric ozone precursors methane (CH_4) and carbon monoxide (CO). Since these substances are also harmful air pollutants, air quality measures that address them might have climate co-benefits.

Scientific evidence and new analyses, including a new assessment by UNEP and the World Meteorological Organization (WMO) (UNEP/WMO 2011), show that controlling black carbon and tropospheric ozone emissions through the rapid implementation of proven emission reduction measures would have immediate and multiple benefits for human well-being. In addition to limiting climate change, reducing SLCF emissions can directly improve human health, food production and the provision of ecosystem services.

Black carbon and tropospheric ozone are two substances that have contributed considerably to warming and regional climate disruption, as well as directly damaging health and crops. However, these substances have not been given priority during the climate change negotiations. One of the key properties of black carbon and tropospheric ozone, as well as of methane (an important greenhouse gas that is also an ozone precursor), is that they have short lifetimes in the atmosphere. The benefits of reducing their concentrations can therefore be achieved in the near term for both climate and air quality-related impacts.

The above mentioned UNEP/WMO assessment provides an overview of the state of science on these two substances. It has also undertaken new analyses to evaluate the benefits of a set of measures identified in the assessment that make use of existing technology. These measures focus on reducing black carbon and ozone precursor emissions (**Table 1**). In evaluating the benefits of their implementation, it is important to take into account their effects on all emissions. The measures in the assessment were identified as those providing 'win-win' benefits for climate as well as for health and crop yields. The assessment finds that if the measures listed in Table 1 were fully implemented globally, they would substantially mitigate near-term global warming, increase world food production, and reduce premature mortality due to outdoor air pollution.

In combination with CO_2 control measures aimed at stabilizing atmospheric greenhouse gas concentrations at 450 parts per million (ppm) CO_2 equivalent, these measures substantially reduce the risk that warming will exceed the 2°C goal agreed at COP 16 in Cancún (**Figure 3**). Keeping below the 2°C level of warming is extremely unlikely without near-term measures to control emissions of both short-lived pollutants and long-lived greenhouse gases, primarily CO_2. Even with all these emission control

Table 1: Identified measures with the potential to significantly reduce near-term climate change and improve air quality

Measure	Sector
BC measures (affecting black carbon and other co-emitted compounds)	
Diesel particle filters for road and off-road vehicles	Transport
Elimination of high-emitting vehicles in road and off-road transport	
Replacing coal by coal briquettes in cooking and heating stoves	Residential
Pellet stoves and boilers, using fuel made from recycled wood waste or sawdust, to replace current wood-burning technologies in the residential sector in industrialized countries	
Introduction of clean-burning biomass stoves for cooking and heating in developing countries	
Substitution of clean-burning cooking stoves using modern fuels for traditional biomass cooking stoves in developing countries	
Replacing traditional brick kilns with vertical shaft kilns and with Hoffman kilns	Industry
Replacing traditional coke ovens with modern recovery ovens, including the improvement of end-of-pipe abatement measures in developing countries	
Ban of open burning of agricultural waste	Agriculture
CH4 measures	
Extended pre-mine degasification and recovery and oxidation of CH4 from ventilation air from coal mines	Extraction and transport of fossil fuel
Extended recovery and utilization, rather than venting, of associated gas and improved control of unintended fugitive emissions from the production of oil and natural gas	
Reduced gas leakage from long-distance transmission pipelines	
Separation and treatment of biodegradable municipal waste through recycling, composting and anaerobic digestion as well as landfill gas collection with combustion/utilization	Waste management
Upgrading primary wastewater treatment to secondary/tertiary treatment with gas recovery and overflow control	
Control of CH4 emissions from livestock, mainly through farm-scale anaerobic digestion of manure from cattle and pigs	Agriculture
Intermittent aeration of continuously flooded rice paddies	

Source: UNEP/WMO (2011)

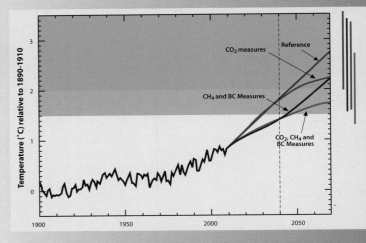

Figure 3: Observed temperatures through 2009 and projected temperatures thereafter under various scenarios, all relative to the 1890-1910 mean. Light and dark green backgrounds indicate zones where projected temperatures are greater than 1.5°C and 2°C, respectively.

Notes: Actual mean temperature observations through 2009, and projected under various scenarios thereafter, are shown relative to the 1890-1910 mean temperature. Estimated ranges for 2070 are shown in the bars on the right. A portion of the uncertainty is common to all scenarios, so that overlapping ranges do not mean there is no difference. For example, if climate sensitivity is large, it is large regardless of the scenario; so temperatures in all scenarios would be towards the high end of their ranges. Source: UNEP/WMO (2011)

measures in place, global mean temperatures would still have a substantial chance of exceeding 2°C towards the end of the century. Thus, further emission reductions could be required if that target, or a more stringent one of 1.5°C, are not to be exceeded.

Warming experienced in different regions varies. Black carbon and tropospheric ozone have made larger contributions to the warming of Arctic surface temperatures since 1890 than they have to the global average. The identified measures could reduce Arctic warming by about 0.7°C (with a range of 0.2-1.3°C) in 2040. This is nearly two-thirds of the estimated 1.1°C warming (with a range of 0.7-1.7°C) projected for the Arctic under the assessment's reference scenario and should substantially decrease the risk of global impacts from changes in this sensitive region, such as sea ice loss (which affects global albedo) and permafrost melt. Black carbon and ozone

in the lower atmosphere also have other major regional climate impacts. For example, they disturb tropical rainfall and regional circulation patterns, such as the Asian monsoon, affecting the livelihoods of millions of people.

Full implementation of the identified measures could avoid 2.4 million premature deaths (within a range of 0.7-4.6 million) and the loss of 52 million tonnes, or 1-4 per cent, of global production of maize, rice, soybean and wheat each year (within a range of 30-140 million tonnes) (**Figure 4**). The greatest benefits will be felt immediately in or near the regions where actions are taken to reduce emissions, with the greatest health and crop benefits expected in Asia. Over 80 per cent of the reduction in mortality due to implementing all the measures will benefit people on that continent.

The benefits of avoided crop yield loss can be attributed equally to measures to reduce methane emissions and measures to reduce those of black carbon. This is because implementing measures to reduce black carbon results in a reduction of ozone precursor emissions that are co-emitted with black carbon. The identified measures in Table 1 are all currently in use in different regions around the world to achieve a variety of environment and development objectives. Much wider and more rapid implementation is required, however, to realize the full benefits identified in the UNEP/WMO assessment.

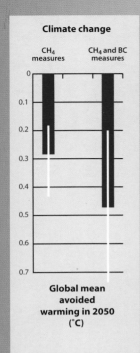

Climate change

Global mean avoided warming in 2050 (°C)

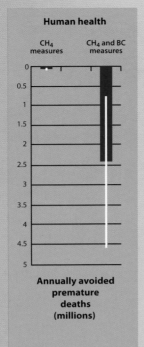

Human health

Annually avoided premature deaths (millions)

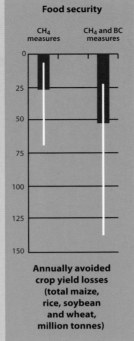

Food security

Annually avoided crop yield losses (total maize, rice, soybean and wheat, million tonnes)

Figure 4: Global impacts of identified emission control measures focusing on methane (CH_4) and black carbon (BC), calculated by taking the average result from running two global climate-composition models, GISS and ECHAM. Benefits are shown with increasing values moving downward, to emphasize that these are reductions in damages.

Notes: The lines on each bar show the range of estimates. They include: for climate change, the range of uncertainty in radiative forcing and climate sensitivity; for human health, uncertainty in concentration-response relationships (for $PM_{2.5}$ and ozone) and in the use of results from different models; and for food security, the range of impacts calculated using ozone changes from different models and uncertainty in exposure-response relationship. Avoided crop yield losses are summed values for the impact of reduced ozone concentrations on wheat, rice, soybean and maize. Source: UNEP/WMO (2011)

Emerging connections between air pollution and human health

Air pollution has long been known to have widespread effects on human health. Poor air quality is associated with increased morbidity and mortality. While it is well established that exposure to atmospheric pollutants can damage the lungs, there is emerging evidence that it may also affect other body systems and is a potential contributor to the increase in autoimmune diseases such as type 1 diabetes, multiple sclerosis and rheumatoid arthritis (Ritz 2010) (**Figure 5**).

Autoimmune diseases are commonly characterized as a group of disorders that target tissues and organs, causing the immune system to be inappropriately activated and to produce destructive responses against self-antigens (that is, constituents of the body's own tissues capable of stimulating autoimmunity).

Particulate matter consists of suspended particulates, the smaller of which are capable of penetrating deep into the respiratory tract and causing significant health damage. Particulates and SO_2 can be emitted from coal-fired power plants without effective emission controls, steel mills, industrial boilers, domestic heating and fossil fuel combustion.

WHO Air Quality Guideline (AQG): annual mean concentrations of no more than 20 µg/m³ for PM_{10} and 10 µg/m³ for $PM_{2.5}$.

Nitrogen dioxide (NO_2) is emitted by motor vehicles, industrial activities, nitrogen fertilizers, fuel and biomass combustion, and aerobic decomposition of organic matter in soils and oceans.

WHO AQG: annual mean concentrations below 40 µg/m³.

Sulphur dioxide (SO_2) is an air pollutant produced when fossil fuels containing sulphur are burned. SO_2 and NO_2 emissions lead to deposition of acid rain and other acidic compounds over long distances, which in turn can lead to leaching of trace minerals and nutrients critical to trees and plants.

WHO AQG: daily mean concentrations of 20 µg/m³.

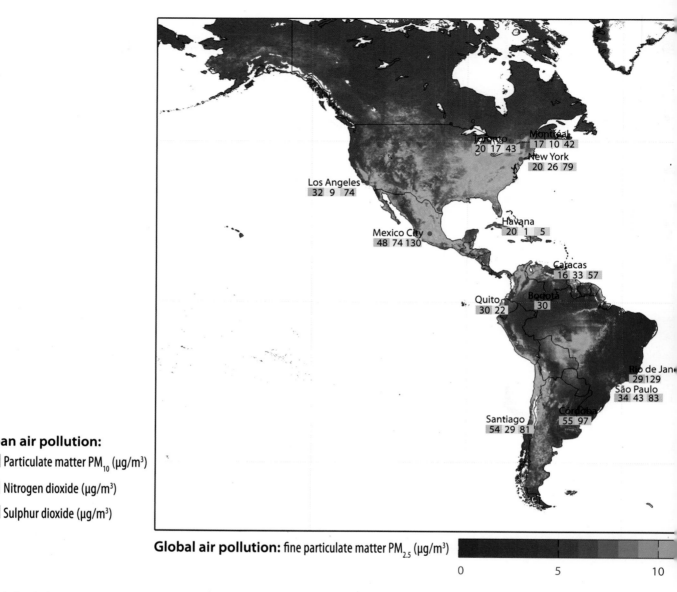

Urban air pollution:

▓ Particulate matter PM$_{10}$ (μg/m³)

░ Nitrogen dioxide (μg/m³)

▒ Sulphur dioxide (μg/m³)

Global air pollution: fine particulate matter PM$_{2.5}$ (μg/m³)

0   5   10

Figure 5: Global and urban airpollution. *Source: Adapted from van Donkelaar et al. (2010) and World Bank (2010)*

The global map shows concentrations of fine particulate matter 2.5 micrometers or less in diameter (PM$_{2.5}$). It was created by combining aerosol measurements from satellite observations between 2001 and 2006 with information about the vertical distribution of aerosols from a computer model. Particularly high PM$_{2.5}$ concentrations are shown in central and eastern Asia.

They exceed 35 micrograms per cubic metre (μg/m³) for 40-50 per cent of the population in that region. Concentrations at this level and higher are associated with an increased risk of mortality of approximately 15 per cent, according to WHO's air quality guidelines (WHO 2006, van Donkelaar et al. 2010).

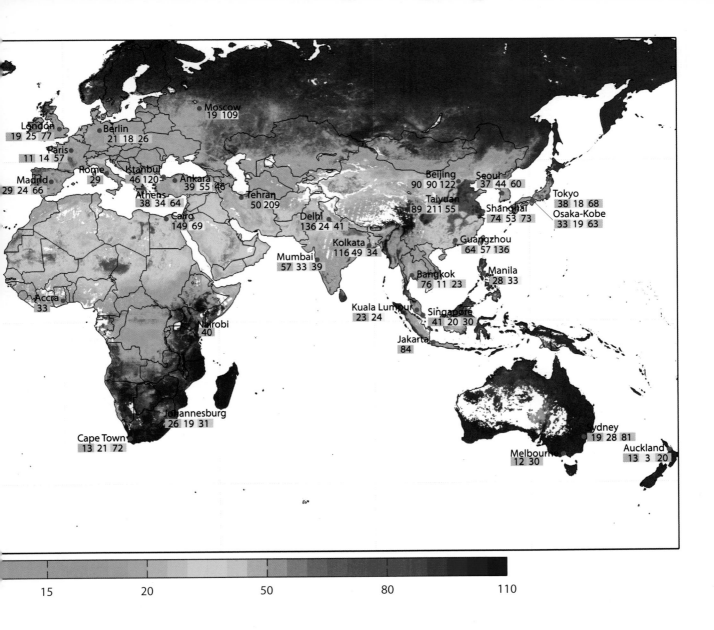

London
19 25 77

Berlin
21 18 26

Paris
11 14 57

Rome
29

Madrid
29 24 66

Istanbul
46 120

Athens
38 34 64

Ankara
39 55 46

Cairo
149 69

Moscow
19 109

Tehran
50 209

Delhi
136 24 41

Kolkata
116 49 34

Mumbai
57 33 39

Beijing
90 90 122

Seoul
37 44 60

Taiyuan
89 211 55

Shanghai
74 53 73

Tokyo
38 18 68

Osaka-Kobe
33 19 63

Guangzhou
64 57 136

Bangkok
76 11 23

Manila
28 33

Kuala Lumpur
23 24

Singapore
41 20 30

Jakarta
84

Accra
33

Nairobi
40

Johannesburg
26 19 31

Cape Town
13 21 72

Sydney
19 28 81

Melbourne
12 30

Auckland
13 3 20

15   20   50   80   110

Air pollution estimates can also represent resident's average annual level of exposure to additional pollutants such as outdoor particulate matter less than 10 micrometers in diameter (PM_{10}), sulphur dioxide (SO_2) and nitrogen dioxide (NO_2). The urban pollutant concentrations shown in the map are sensitive to local conditions and can differ within the same urban area. Data on particulate matter are often estimated as average annual concentrations in residential areas, away from air pollution 'hotspots' such as industrial districts and transport corridors. The SO_2 and NO_2 concentration data are based on average observed concentrations at urban monitoring sites (World Bank 2010).

Warming lakes

Water in many of the world's largest lakes is warming as a result of climate change (**Figure 6**). This is the outcome of a 25-year survey of the surface water temperatures of 167 of the largest lakes using satellite data (Schneider and Hook 2010). In each decade temperatures have increased by 0.45°C on average. In some lakes they rose by 1°C. Although this may seem a modest upward trend, even small increases in temperature can have dramatic effects on water quality and ecosystems in lakes. For example, they can induce algal blooms, enhance the risk that invasive species will become established, or cause shifts in plant and fish populations. Since much aquatic life is confined within the boundaries of lakes, options to migrate to other, cooler habitats are limited. Further warming could therefore result in rapid biodiversity loss in freshwater ecosystems.

Most scientists have used air temperature mainly to monitor climate change. Monitoring warming trends in lakes may be a new way to assess the impacts of global climate change on Earth.

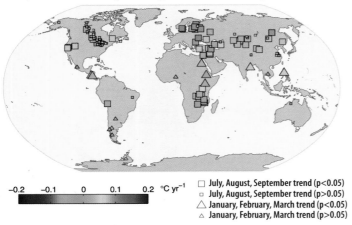

| −0.2 | −0.1 | 0 | 0.1 | 0.2 | °C yr⁻¹ |

□ July, August, September trend (p<0.05)
▫ July, August, September trend (p>0.05)
△ January, February, March trend (p<0.05)
▵ January, February, March trend (p>0.05)

Figure 6: Worldwide trends in nighttime lake surface temperature derived from satellite data. *Source: Schneider and Hook (2010)*

Biodiversity under threat—time to act

2010 was the International Year of Biodiversity. A significant intergovernmental agreement was reached in Nagoya, Japan, in October at the Conference of the Parties to the Convention on Biological Diversity (COP 10), when governments agreed to renew their pledge to reduce the global rate of biodiversity loss. The new ten-year Strategic Plan, which replaces the previous, unachieved target of halting biodiversity loss by 2010, will guide international and national efforts. Among its targets is at least halving and, where feasible, bringing close to zero the rate of loss of natural habitats, including forests, and protecting 17 per cent of land and inland waters and 10 per cent of coastal and marine areas by 2020. Currently, 13 per cent of land and less than 1 per cent of oceans are protected for conservation. The meeting also agreed on the Nagoya Protocol on access to and sharing of benefits from the use of the planet's genetic resources. This international protocol provides a framework for access to genetic resources based on prior informed consent and mutually agreed terms, with fair and equitable sharing of benefits and in consideration of traditional knowledge. The protocol is expected to enter into force by 2012 (CBD 2010).

Monitoring data confirm that biodiversity is more than ever under threat. According to a recent report, over 22 per cent of the world's plants are at risk of extinction, in large part due to loss of habitats through conversion of natural areas for agricultural use, including food and biofuel production. Regions where plants are under the greatest threat include South East Asia, Brazil (Mata Atlântica), Australasia, Madagascar and Europe (IUCN 2010).

A survey by the Global Environment Facility (GEF) shows that biodiversity conservation is one of countries' key environmental concerns. It also identifies lack of comprehensive and adequate environmental policies and weak legislative and regulatory instruments as reasons for limited improvement in environmental management (GEF 2010) (**Figure 7**).

New policy responses to the need for biodiversity conservation aim to make biodiversity values increasingly visible, thus encouraging more efficient use as well as conservation. Society's willingness to pay to conserve particular species or landscapes, for example for food or wood production, have traditionally informed economic valuations of nature. Intangible values, which are often not reflected, vary according to local biophysical and ecological circumstances and social, economic and cultural contexts.

A change in thinking is needed, so that decision makers and other stakeholders will regard ecosystem conservation and restoration as a viable investment option that can support a range of policy goals including food security, urban development, water purification and wastewater treatment, regional development, and climate change mitigation and adaptation (TEEB 2010). Brazil, India and Japan are three countries that are taking steps to incorporate an ecosystem service approach which can identify both the benefits and costs of conserving or restoring nature. India has already announced plans to develop and implement a framework for green national accounts by 2015.

Engaging citizens in biodiversity programmes can foster awareness and enhance the policy process. With 2 billion people online and 90 per cent of the world population using mobile phones (ITU 2010), new opportunities to participate in biodiversity conservation efforts are arising.

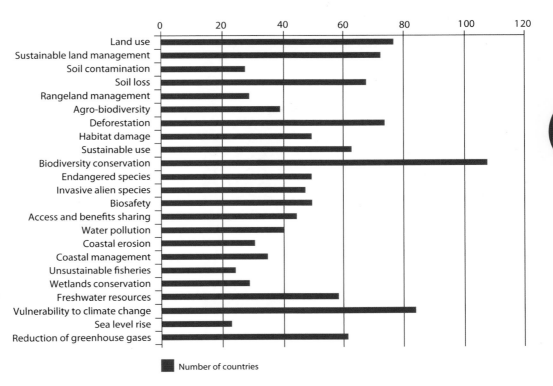

Figure 7: Countries' priority environmental concerns. Out of 119 countries participating in the GEF National Capacity Self-Assessments (NCSA) survey, more than 100 identified biodiversity conservation as a priority environmental concern. *Source: GEF (2010)*

Number of countries

A new international body, the Intergovernmental Platform on Biodiversity and Ecosystem Services (IPBES), was formally approved by the United Nations General Assembly in December. It will work to bridge scientific knowledge on biodiversity decline and ecosystem degradation with knowledge related to the effective policy solutions and responses required to reverse damaging trends (UNEP 2010c and d). *Credit: Conrad Savy*

Getting involved: citizen science

Participation by the general public in scientific research—sometimes referred to as 'citizen science'—can help raise awareness and foster local engagement in decision making. It can also assist with the collection of valuable data. In particular, citizen science has considerable potential to engage stakeholders in addressing complex and dynamic issues such as biodiversity conservation (**Box 3**).

The global problem of biodiversity loss is related to local issues such as urbanization, infrastructure development, expansion of agriculture, and overfishing. Local commitment can therefore help integrate biodiversity concerns in planning decisions and halt the trend of plant and animal species loss. In addition, there is an urgent need for biodiversity data, as incomplete coverage of spatial and taxonomical indicators makes it difficult to obtain an accurate overview of the state of biodiversity (Butchart et al. 2010). Satellites and other common remote sensing techniques allow estimates of the extent and productivity of different ecosystems and of species diversity—in the case of tree cover, for example. However, such techniques are not suitable for assessments of variations in many of the components of biological diversity. In the case of most ecological groups, such as birds, butterflies or amphibians, human observers are needed for species sampling and recognition, whereas automatic devices can be used and combined to estimate the diversity patterns of micro-organisms (Couvet et al. 2008).

Volunteer monitoring schemes can integrate the collection of basic data with daily activities, such as fishing (Levrel et al. 2010). Using state-of-the-art survey designs or data-analysis methods, these schemes provide relatively reliable data and therefore yield unbiased results. The quality of the data collected by volunteers is more likely to be determined by survey design, analytical methodology and communication skills within schemes than by involvement of volunteers in itself (Schmeller et al. 2009).

According to a European survey, there are 623 schemes for monitoring species and habitats, with volunteer involvement spread over 35 European countries and participation by more than 100 000 volunteers. In particular, species monitoring schemes such as bird counts involve a high level of volunteers compared to professionals (EuMon 2010). Almost half these schemes are funded nationally (47 per cent), one-third (sub)regionally, and 11 per cent privately. Scientific grants account for only 4 per cent of funding, although scientific interest is the main reason for launching such schemes (**Figure 8**).

In France there are monitoring schemes, developed and operated by scientists, in which volunteers provide 75 per cent of full-time staffing. A recent study suggests that species monitoring currently carried out by French volunteers would cost US$0.8 million to 5.3 million per year if professionals were hired instead (Levrel et al. 2010).

Citizen monitoring schemes can also enhance the policy process. Schemes that involve local people, and directly assess environmental resource changes that impact them, are often very effective at influencing resource management decisions and can reduce the time it takes for decisions to be implemented (Danielsen et al. 2010). Nevertheless, the potential for locally based monitoring schemes remains largely unexplored in developing countries. Funding constraints and limited expertise are significant constraints in these countries while biodiversity is often richer, and people are more directly dependent on natural resources, than in developed ones (Danielsen et al. 2008).

Integrated species-monitoring programmes for selected land animals, butterflies and plants can be initiated with modest financial assistance. It is estimated that it would cost about US$50 000 per country per year to develop pilot projects with the goal of providing rigorous population trends for selected species by 2020 in regions which are currently under-monitored, such as sub-Saharan Africa, South America and East Asia (Pereira et al. 2010).

New opportunities to observe the environment are also emerging due to the rapid development of mobile sensing technology (Sutherland et al. 2010) (**Box 4**). Users can register

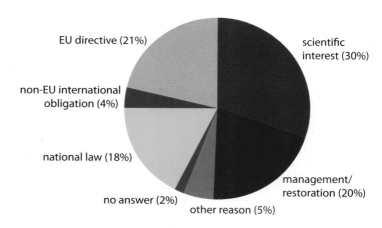

Figure 8: Reasons for launching volunteer monitoring schemes in Europe, expressed as percentages. Most European species and habitat monitoring schemes are set up for scientific purposes (30 per cent). To a lesser extent, they are launched to comply with EU directives, national laws or international obligations. One-fifth of the schemes aim directly at habitat management and restoration. *Source: EuMon (2010)*

A volunteer in Project PteroCount uses a bat detector at a monitoring site. Monitoring animals such as the Nepalese myotis bat shown here (*Myotis nipalensis*) on a regular basis helps determine population trends. *Credit: Sanjan Thapa*

Box 3: Get involved in citizen science programmes on biodiversity

Earthdive: Global Dive Log containing observational data on key indicator species and human induced pressures of value in marine conservation. United Nations Environment Programme-World Conservation Monitoring Centre (UNEP-WCMC): www.earthdive.com

Project PteroCount: South Asian Bat Monitoring Programme. Zoo Outreach Organisation/Wildlife Information Liaison Development/ Chiroptera Conservation and Information Network of South Asia: www.pterocount.org/index.html

REEFCHECK: Monitoring and conservation of tropical coral reefs and California rocky reefs. Reef Check Foundation: http://reefcheck.org/

South American Wildlands Mapping: Mapping and analysis of roadless/undeveloped areas in Chile and Argentina. Pacific Biodiversity Institute: www.pacificbio.org/helpout/volunteer-south-america.html

Treewatch: Observing and recording changes in the health of an adopted tree. Sylva Foundation: http://sylva.org.uk/treewatch/

sound, pictures, videos, Global Positioning System co-ordinates and other data. Such data can then be uploaded directly to the internet via mobile networks providing real-time data and be used for monitoring of, for example, the environmental situation during and after natural disasters or monitoring of pollinators and wildlife sensing. A recently launched educational programme makes it possible for young people in many countries to survey 9 hectares of tropical forest remotely. Participants report changes observed in their allocated area of the forest directly on a server portal.

Box 4: Innovative mobile phone monitoring

Innovative mobile phone technologies and applications save lives in disaster areas. Portals help connect people to resources to aid disaster recovery and engage stakeholders in problem solving. *Ushahidi*—which means 'testimony' in Swahili—software used for this purpose was initially developed to map reports of violence in Kenya following the 2008 elections. Information was exchanged via SMS and reports were verified by administrators. Similarly, information provided by citizens helped to identify needs in flood-hit areas of Pakistan in 2010 and determine the precise locations of displacements. An example is Pakreport, set up by a group of individuals soon after the floods began in July. Another service established by USAid allowed people to share the latest information and updates on recovery efforts via SMS. In Pakistan, which has more than 99 million mobile phone subscribers out of a total population of 170 million, there is a very high level of accessibility (IRIN 2010).

Sustainable agricultural development

Food security remained a concern in 2010, as rising global food consumption, changing diets and climate vulnerability placed stresses on production. World wheat production is projected to increase by 1.5 million tonnes in 2010/11, compared with an increase in wheat consumption of 2.5 million tonnes (USDA 2010). Thirty-six of the 50 countries whose food supplies are most at risk due to extreme droughts, high poverty rates, and poor infrastructure for transporting agricultural products are in Africa, particularly sub-Saharan Africa (Maplecroft 2010b). Looking back at 2007/2008, analysis shows that increasing oil prices, greater demand for biofuels and export restrictions, among other factors, affected world cereal prices and contributed to the global food crisis (Heady and Fan 2010).

World food production needs to increase by 70 per cent to feed an expected world population of more than 9 billion by 2050 (ID2E 2010). In addition, the world's primary biomass demand is projected to increase to 1 604-1 952 million tonnes of oil equivalent by 2030 depending on the availability of surplus agricultural land (OECD/IEA 2010). Agriculture provides a livelihood for 75 per cent of the poor in developing countries. Furthermore, over one-third of direct global carbon emissions are due to agriculture and other land use changes. This share is projected to increase in coming decades. It is estimated that agriculture has the potential to sequester up to 90 per cent of its total carbon emissions (ARDD 2010). The challenge is to find ways to use natural resources in agriculture, forestry and fisheries sustainably without depleting them.

The first Global Conference on Agriculture, Food Security and Climate Change, held in The Hague, the Netherlands, in November 2010, provided a forum where policy makers discussed practical solutions that can achieve triple wins: climate change adaptation, mitigation and food security. It will take a variety of tools to improve existing land practices and husbandry and sequester carbon in soils and plant biomass. They include restoration of degraded agricultural landscapes, water conservation and harvesting, pest and disease control, soil and nutrient management, conservation and maintenance of crop diversity through contributions to benefit-sharing mechanisms, efficient harvesting and early transformation of agricultural products to reduce post-harvest losses, energy conservation and waste minimization (ID2E 2010). The successful recovery of desertified land in China is an example of how desertification can be reversed and reclaimed land put back into agricultural production (**Box 5**).

Millet harvested in Niger. Enhanced agroforestry schemes in Africa have benefited the environment, farmers and food security. In Niger over 4.8 million hectares of millet and sorghum are being grown on land where agroforestry is practised. *Source: ARDD (2010). Credit: USDA/FAS/OGA*

Box 5: Reversing desertification in Ningxia, China

The Ningxia Hui Autonomous Region in northwest China is one of the country's driest and least developed areas. Ningxia mainly consists of sandy land, desert steppe and shifting sands. Around 8 770 000 hectares, or 57 per cent of the region's total land area, has experienced desertification, land degradation and shifting sands, affecting over 3 million people or approximately 60 per cent of Ningxia's population. Some 1 320 000 hectares of agricultural land and 1 210 000 hectares of desert steppe and grassland, associated with more than 600 villages, are at risk of further desertification.

However, Ningxia is also one of the areas where desertified land has successfully been recovered for agriculture. A desertification management approach that combines regulations, changes in administrative procedures, sustainable development incentives and public-private partnerships has increased the amount of land under cultivation. This approach also contributes to the development of a green economy and to job creation. Besides the activities of farmers, individual households and others, 'green enterprises' have been taking part in reforestation, the planting of vineyards, herbal medicines and apple orchards, and the construction of wineries and an apple juice factory.

Farmers in Ningxia are encouraged to practise conservation agriculture and nutrient management. The area on which cash crops such as grapes, melons, Chinese wolfberries and apricots are being grown has increased, and growing Chinese ephedra plants used in traditional medicine is encouraged. The methods used to protect plants in Ningxia's harsh arid climate include bans on open grazing by sheep and goats and on the collection of wild herbs and edible black moss (Flagelliform nostoc).

Large-scale projects to reverse desertification in Ningxia include the Shapotou dam on the Yellow River, irrigation schemes, and the construction of more than 200 000 hectares of artificial oases, where over 200 000 migrants from desertification-prone areas are being resettled. In the county of Yanchi alone, 293 000 hectares have been planted with trees, shrubs and grasses, 33 000 hectares of moving sand dunes have been stabilized, and 80 000 hectares of degraded desert steppe and grassland have been revegetated and rehabilitated.

To reclaim desertified areas and protect them from further erosion, sustainable agriculture and sustainable land management are essential. In the context of mitigating land degradation and drought disaster risk management, Ningxia is also focusing on water resources management and biodiversity conservation in drylands and arid zones.

Source: Government of Ningxia Hui Autonomous Region (2010)

Grapes and other fruits, vegetables, cereals and medicinal plants are grown on reclaimed land. Ningxia's new vineyards and wineries are creating jobs as well as helping to control desertification. *Credit: Ningxia Forest Bureau*

Sand barriers made of straw and rolled reeds are widely used to combat desertification in China. Semi-buried, and arranged in a checkerboard pattern, they stabilize the sand surface. Other techniques include planting grasses, shrubs and trees, excavating buried soils, and irrigation. *Credit: Ningxia Forest Bureau*

References

ARDD (2010). There is no climate security without food security and no food security without climate security. Agriculture and Rural Development Day. Statement. Saturday December 4, Cancun, Mexico. http://ccafs.cgiar.org/blog/there-no-climate-security-without-food-security-and-no-food-security-without-climate-security

Barbier, E. (2009). A Global Green New Deal: Rethinking the Economic Recovery. Report prepared for the Economics and Trade Branch, Division of Technology, Industry and Economics, United Nations Environment Programme. http://www.unep.ch/greeneconomy/portals/30/docs/GGND-Report-April2009.pdf

Brown, L.R. (2009). Plan B 4.0: Mobilizing to Save Civilization. Earth Policy Institute. http://www.earth-policy.org/images/uploads/book_files/pb4book.pdf

Butchart, S. H. M., Stuart, H. M., Walpole, M., Collen, B., van Strien, A. etv al. (2010). Global Biodiversity: Indicators of Recent Declines. Science, 328 (5982), 1164-1168

CBD (Convention on Biological Diversity) (2010). A new era of living in harmony with Nature is born at the Nagoya Biodiversity Summit. Press release http://www.cbd.int/doc/press/2010/pr-2010-10-29-cop-10-en.pdf

Couvet, D., Jiguet, F., Julliard, R., Levrel, H. and Teyssedre, A. (2008). Enhancing citizen contributions to biodiversity science and public policy. Interdisciplinary Science Reviews, 33(1), 95-103. http://www.unesco.org/mab/doc/euromab/2009/isr.pdf

Danielsen, F., Burgess, N.D., Balmford, A., Donald, P.F., Funder, M., Jones, J.P.G., Alviola, P., Balete, D.S., Blombey, T., Brashares, J., Child, B., Enghoff, M., Fjeldså, J., Holt, S., Hübertz, H., Jensen, A.E., Jensen, P.M., Massao, J., Mendoza, M.M., Ngaga, Y., Poulsen, M.K., Rueda, R., Sam, M., Skielboe, T., Stuart-Hill, G., Topp-Jørgensen, E. and Yonten, D. (2008). Local Participation in Natural Resource Monitoring: A Characterization of Approaches. Conservation Biology, 23(1), 31-42.

Danielsen, F., Burgess, N.D., Jensen, P.M., Pirhofer-Walzl, K. (2010). Environmental monitoring: the scale and speed of implementation varies according to the degree of peoples involvement. Journal of Applied Ecology, 47(6), 1166-1168

EuMon (2010). EU-wide monitoring methods and systems of surveillance for species and habitats of Community interest. http://eumon.ckff.si/index1.php

G20 Seoul Summit (2010). The Seoul Summit Document. http://www.g20.utoronto.ca/2010/g20seoul-doc.pdf

GEF (Global Environment Facility) (2010). National Capacity Self-Assessments: Results and Lessons Learned for Global Environmental Sustainability. http://www.thegef.org/gef/sites/thegef.org/files/publication/NCSA-SR-web-100913.pdf

Gershenfled, N., Samouhos, S. and Nordman, B. (2010). Intelligent Infrastructure for Energy Efficiency. Science, 327 (5969), 1086-1088

Global Conference on Agriculture, Food Security and Climate Change, The Hague, the Netherlands, 31 October-5 November 2010. Chair's Summary. http://www.afcconference.com/final-roadmap-for-action

Government of Ningxia Hui Autonomous Region (2010). Governmental Guiding, Projects Motivating and Public Participation to Push forward the Progress Combating Desertification. Summary Report Combating Desertification in Ningxia

Headey, D. and Fan, S. (2010). Reflections on the global food crisis : how did it happen? how has it hurt? and how can we prevent the next one? IFPRI research monograph

ID2E (2010). Global Conference on Agriculture, Food Security and Climate Change, the Hague, the Netherlands, 31 October-5 November 2010. Chair's Summary. www.afcconference.com/final-roadmap-for-action

IEA (International Energy Agency) (2010a). Energy Technology Perspectives 2010. Scenarios and Strategies to 2050. Executive Summary. http://www.iea.org/techno/etp/etp10/English.pdf

IEA (2010b). World Energy Outlook 2010. Presentation to the press. London, 9 November 2010. http://www.worldenergyoutlook.org/docs/weo2010/weo2010_london_nov9.pdf

IISD (International Institute for Sustainable Development) (2010). A report of the High-level Plenary Meeting of the 65th Session of the UN General Assembly on the Millennium Development Goals (MDGs). MDG Summit Bulletin, 153, 9. http://www.iisd.ca/download/pdf/sd/ymbvol153num9e.pdf

IRIN (2010). Using SMS to pinpoint humanitarian needs. IRIN News 28 September www.irinnews.org/report.aspx?ReportId=90602

IPCC (2007). The physical science basis: contribution of working group 1 to the Fourth Assessment Report of the Intergovernmental Panel on Climate Change, Cambridge University Press, New York

ITU (International Telecommunication Union) (2010). The World in 2010. The Rise of 3G, Geneva

IUCN (International Union for Conservation of Nature) (2010). Plants under pressure: A global assessment. The first report of the IUCN Sampled Red List Index for Plants. Royal Botanic Gardens, Kew, UK. http://www.kew.org/ucm/groups/public/documents/document/kppcont_027694.pdf

Levrel, H., Fontaine, B., Henry, P., Jiguet, F., Julliard, R., Kerbiriou, C. and Couvet, D. (2010). Balancing state and volunteer investment in biodiversity monitoring for the implementation of CBD indicators: A French example. Ecological Economics, 69(7), 1580-1586

Maplecroft (2010a). Index of 350 biggest US companies reveals relationship between climate innovation and financial performance. http://www.maplecroft.com/about/news/cii.html

Maplecroft (2010b). African nations dominate Macplecroft's new Food Security Risk index – China and Russia will face challenges. http://www.maplecroft.com/about/news/food-security.html

Molina, M., Zaelke, D., Sarma, K.M., Andersen, S.O., Ramanathan, V. And Kaniaru, D. Reducing abrupt climate change risk using the Montreal Protocol and other regulatory actions to complement cuts in CO_2 emissions. Proceedings of the National Academy of Sciences, 106(49), 20616-20621

OECD/IEA (2010). Sustainable Production of Second-Generation Biofuels. Potential and perspectives in major economies and developing countries. Information Paper. Organisation for Economic Co-operation and Development/International Energy Agency, Paris

Pereira, M.H., Belnap, J., Brummitt, N., Collen, B., Ding, H., Gonzalez-Espinosa, M., Gregory, R.D., Honrado, J., Jongman, R.H.G., Julliard, R., McRae, L., Proença, V., Rodrigues, P., Opige, M., Rodriguez, J.P., Schmeller, D.S., van Swaay, C. and Vieira, C. (2010). Global biodiversity monitoring. Frontiers in Ecology and the Environment, 8, 459-460

Red Cross (2010). In the news 2010. http://www.redcross.org/portal/site/en/

REN 21 (2010). Renewables 2010 Global Status Report. REB 21 Secretariat. Paris, France

Ritz, S. A. (2010). Air pollution as a potential contributor to the 'epidemic' of autoimmune disease. Medical Hypotheses, 74, 110-117

Schmeller, D.S., Henry, P., Julliard, R., Gruber, B., Clobert, J., Dziock, F., Lengyel, S., Nowicki, P., Déri, E., Budrys, E., Kull, T., Tali, K., Bauch, B., Settele, J., van Swaay, C., Kobler, A., Babij, V., Papastergiadou, E. and Henle, K. (2009). Advantages of Volunteer-Based Biodiversity Monitoring in Europe. Conservation Biology, 23(2), 307-316

Schneider, P. and Hook, S.J. (2010). Space observations of inland water bodies show rapid surface warming since 1985. Geophysical Research Letters, 37(22), L22405

Sutherlands, J.W., Clout, M., Cote, I.M., Daszak, P., Depledge, M.H. et al. (2010) Conservation Issues for 2010 Trends in Ecology and Evolution, 25, 1-7

TEEB (The Economics of Ecosystems and Biodiversity) (2010). The Economics of Ecosystems and Biodiversity: Mainstreaming the Economics of Nature: A synthesis of the approach, conclusions and recommendations of TEEB. http://www.teebweb.org/LinkClick.aspx?fileticket=bYhDohL_TuM%3D&tabid=924&mid=1813

UN (United Nations) (2010a). High-level Plenary Meeting on the Millennium Development Goals. Keeping the promise: a forward-looking review to promote an agreed action agenda to achieve the Millennium Development Goals by 2015. Compilation of Partnership Events and Action Commitments. http://www.un.org/en/mdg/summit2010/pdf/HLPM__Side%20events_CRP.pdf

UN (United Nations) (2010b). The Millennium Development Goals Report 2010. http://www.un.org/millenniumgoals/pdf/MDG%20Report%202010%20En%20r15%20-low%20res%2020100615%20-.pdf

UNEP (2010a). UN Climate Change Conference in Cancun delivers balanced package of decisions, restores faith in multilateral process. Press Release. www.unep.org/Documents.Multilingual/Default.asp?DocumentID=653&ArticleID=6866&l=en

UNEP (2010b). The Emissions Gap Report: Are the Copenhagen Accord Pledges Sufficient to limit Global Warming to 2℃ or 1.5℃? United Nations Environment Programme, Nairobi

UNEP (2010c). Report of the third ad hoc intergovernmental and multi-stakeholder meeting on an intergovernmental science-policy platform on biodiversity and ecosystem services. Busan, Republic of Korea, 7 -11 June 2010

UNEP (2010d). Biodiversity Year Ends on a High Note as UN General Assembly Backs Resolution Signing into Life an 'IPCC for Nature'. Press release, 21 Dec. http://www.unep.org/Documents.Multilingual/Default.asp?DocumentID=653&ArticleID=6872&l=en

UNEP/WMO (in press). Integrated assessment of black carbon and tropospheric ozone. United Nations Environment Programme, Nairobi

UNEP and Bloomberg New Energy Finance (2010). Global Trends in Sustainable Energy Investment 2010. Analysis of Trends and Issues in the Financing of Renewable Energy and Energy Efficiency. United Nations Environment Programme, Paris

UNFCCC (2007). Dialogue on long-term cooperative action to address climate change by enhancing implementation of the Convention. UNFCCC, Bonn

UNGA (United Nations General Assembly) (2010). Keeping the Promise: United to Achieve the Millennium Development Goals. Draft Resolution Referred to the High-level Plenary Meeting of the Genera Assembly by the General Assembly at its sixty-fourth session. http://www.un.org/en/mdg/summit2010/pdf/mdg%20outcome%20document.pdf

USDA (United States Department of Agriculture) (2010). World Agricultural Supply and Demand Estimates, 9 Nov. http://www.usda.gov/oce/commodity/wasde/latest.pdf

US EPA (2011). Climate Change - Health and Environmental Effects. United States Environmental Protection Agency http://www.epa.gov/climatechange/effects/health.html#air

Velders, G.J.M., Andersen, O.S., Daniel, J.S., Fahey, D.W. and McFarland, M. (2007). The importance of the Montreal Protocol in protecting climate. Proceedings of the National Academy of Sciences of the United States of America, 104(12), 4814-4819

van Donkelaar, A., Martin, R.V., Brauer, M., Kahn, R., Levy, R, Verduzco, C. and Villeneuve, P.J. (2010). Global Estimates of Ambient Fine Particulate Matter Concentrations from Satellite-Based Aerosol Optical Depth: Development and Application. Environmental Health Perspectives. 118(6), 847-855

WBCSD (2010). WBCSD emphasizes need for public private cooperation to find solutions for climate change challenges. world Business Council for Sustainable Development. Press Release. 6 September. www.wbcsd.org/plugins/DocSearch/details.asp?type=DocDet&ObjectId=Mzg2Mzk

WHO (2006). WHO Air quality guidelines for particulate matter, ozone, nitrogen dioxide and sulfur dioxide. Global update 2005. Summary of risk assessment. World Health Organization, Geneva

WMO (2011). Press Release No. 906. http://www.wmo.int/pages/mediacentre/press_releases/pr_906_en.html

World Bank (2010). World Development Indicators 2010. World Bank. Washington, D.C.

Upcoming events 2011

10-11 January
First Intersessional Meeting for UN Conference on Sustainable Development (UNCSD), also called Rio+20, New York, United States
www.uncsd2012.org/

11-12 January
First Sustainable Infrastructure Financing Summit, Basel, Switzerland
http://globalenergybasel.com/programme-and-slides-geb-2011/

24-28 January
Second Session of the Intergovernmental Negotiating Committee to Prepare a Global Legally Binding Instrument on Mercury (INC2), Chiba, Japan
www.unep.org/hazardoussubstances/Mercury/Negotiations/INC2/tabid/3468/language/en-US/Default.aspx

24 January-4 February
Ninth Session of the UN Forum on Forests (UNFF 9)/ Launch of the International Year of Forests 2011, UNFF Secretariat, UN Headquarters, New York, United States
www.un.org/esa/forests/session.html

26 January-30 January
Davos World Economic Forum, 'Shared Norms for the New Reality', Davos, Switzerland
www.weforum.org/events/world-economic-forum-annual-meeting-2011

2 February
Opening for signature of the Nagoya Protocol on Access to Genetic Resources and the Fair and Equitable Sharing of Benefits Arising from their Utilization to the Convention on Biological Diversity, United Nations Headquarters, New York, United States
www.cbd.int/meetings/

3-5 February
Phosphorus, Food and Our Future: Sustainable Phosphorus Summit, Arizona State University, Tempe Campus, Tempe, United States
http://sols.asu.edu/frontiers/2011/index.php

10-11 February
Organisation for Economic Cooperation and Development (OECD) Green Growth Strategy Workshop, OECD Headquarters, Paris, France
https://www.oecd.org/document/56/0,3343,en_2649_37465_46328312_1_1_1_1,00.html

14-18 February
Regular process for global reporting and assessment of the state of the marine environment, including socio-economic aspects (Regular Process), Meeting of the General Assembly Ad Hoc Working Group of the Whole, UN Headquarters, New York, United States
www.un.org/Depts/los/global_reporting/global_reporting.htm

21-24 February
Twenty-sixth Session of the UNEP Governing Council/Global Ministerial Environment Forum, Nairobi, Kenya
www.unep.org/gc/gc26/

28 February-4 March
Intergovernmental Preparatory Meeting for the Nineteenth Session of the Commission on Sustainable Development (CSD 19), UN Headquarters, New York, United States
www.un.org/esa/dsd/csd/csd_csd19_ipm.shtml

7-8 March
Second PrepCom for UN Conference on Sustainable Development (Rio+20), Division for Sustainable Development, UN Headquarters, New York, United States
www.un.org/esa/dsd/index.shtml

14-18 March
Climate Investment Funds (CIF) Partnership Forum, Tunis, Tunisia
www.climateinvestmentfunds.org/cif/partnership_forum_2011_home

14-18 March
Pacific Climate Change Roundtable, Alofi, Niue
www.sprep.org/event/

20-25 March
Fifth International Marine Debris Conference, Honolulu, Hawaii, United States
www.5IMDC.org

3-5 April
First Session of the International Renewable Energy Agency (IRENA) Assembly and Fifth Preparatory Commission for IRENA, Abu Dhabi, United Arab Emirates
www.irena.org/

25-29 April
Fifth Meeting of the Conference of the Parties to the Stockholm Convention on Persistent Organic Pollutants (POPs), Geneva, Switzerland
http://chm.pops.int/default.aspx

2-13 May
Nineteenth Session of the Commission on Sustainable Development (CSD 19), UN Headquarters, New York, United States
www.un.org/esa/dsd/csd/csd_csd19.shtml

10-13 May
Thirty-third Session of the Intergovernmental Panel on Climate Change (IPCC 33), Abu Dhabi, United Arab Emirates
www.ipcc.ch/calendar_of_meetings/calendar_of_meetings.shtml

14-18 May
Second International Marine Conservation Congress, IMCC 2, Making Marine Science Matter, Victoria, Canada
www.conbio.org/IMCC2011/

WORLD ENVIRONMENT DAY

UNEP

5 JUNE
Forests: Nature at Your Service
In support of the UN International Year of Forests

5 June
World Environment Day, 'Forests: Nature at Your Service', Delhi, India
www.unep.org/wed/

20-22 June
Joint IPCC Expert Meeting of WGI, WGII and WGIII on Geoengineering, Lima, Peru
www.ipcc-wg2.gov/meetings/EMs/index.html#5

20-22 June
Vienna Energy Conference 2011: Energy for All – Time for Action, Vienna, Austria
www.unido.org/index.php?id=1001185

20-24 June
Fifth Meeting of the Conference of the Parties to the Rotterdam Convention on Prior Informed Consent (PIC COP 5), Geneva, Switzerland
www.pic.int/

11-15 July
Sixty-second Session of the Marine Environment Protection Committee, International Maritime Organization, IMO Headquarters, London, United Kingdom
www.imo.org/MediaCentre/MeetingSummaries/Pages/Default.aspx

16-22 July
Thirteenth Regular Session of the Commission on Genetic Resources for Food and Agriculture (CGRFA 13), FAO Headquarters, Rome, Italy
www.fao.org/nr/cgrfa/cgrfa-home/en/

29 August-2 September 2011
Intersessional Ad Hoc Open-Ended Working Group of the International Conference on Chemicals Management (ICCM OEWG), Belgrade, Serbia
www.saicm.org/index.php?content=meeting&mid=124&menuid=&def=1

8-12 September
Second World Biodiversity Congress, Kuching, Malaysia
www.worldbiodiversity2011.com/

13 September
Opening of the Sixty-sixth Session of the UN General Assembly, UN Headquarters, New York, United States
www.un.org/en/ga/

20 September
UN General Assembly high-level event on 'Addressing desertification, land degradation and drought in the context of sustainable development and poverty eradication', UN Headquarters, New York, United States
www.unccd.int/

21-23 September
Seventh 'Environment for Europe' Ministerial Conference, Astana, Kazakhstan
www.unece.org/env/efe/Astana/welcome.html

10-21 October
UN Convention to Combat Desertification in Those Countries Experiencing Serious Drought and/or Desertification, Particularly in Africa (UNCCD) and the tenth session of the Conference of the Parties, UNCCD COP 10, Changwon City, Republic of Korea
www.unccd.int/cop/cop10/menu.php

17-21 October
Tenth Meeting of the Conference of the Parties to the Basel Convention on the Control of Transboundary Movements of Hazardous Wastes and their Disposal, Cartagena, Colombia
www.basel.int/meetings/meetings.html

30 October-4 November 2011
Third Session of the Intergovernmental Negotiating Committee to Prepare a Global Legally Binding Instrument on Mercury (INC 3), Ouagadougou, Burkina Faso
www.unep.org/hazardoussubstances/MercuryNot/MercuryNegotiations/tabid/3320/language/en-US/Default.aspx

14-15 November
Second Intersessional Meeting for UN Conference on Sustainable Development (UNCSD), also called Rio+20, UN Headquarters, New York, United States
www.uncsd2012.org/

14-18 November
Joint Ninth Conference of the Parties to the Vienna Convention and Twenty-third Meeting of the Parties to the Montreal Protocol, Bali, Indonesia
http://ozone.unep.org/Events/meetings2011.shtml

28 November-9 December
Seventeenth Session of the Conference of the Parties to the United Nations Framework Convention on Climate Change (UNFCCC) (COP 17) and seventh session of the Meeting of the Parties to the Kyoto Protocol (COP/MOP 7), Durban, South Africa
http://unfccc.int/meetings/unfccc_calendar/items/2655.php

Antarctic fur seal entangled in plastic sheeting. *Credit: British Antarctic Survey*

Plastic Debris in the Ocean

Every year large amounts of plastic debris enter the ocean, where it slowly fragments and accumulates in convergence zones. Scientists are concerned about the possible impacts of small plastic fragments—microplastics—in the environment. The role of plastics as a vector for transporting chemicals and species in the ocean is as yet poorly understood, but it is a potential threat to ecosystems and human health. Improved waste management is the key to preventing plastic and other types of litter from entering the ocean.

The ocean has become a global repository for much of the waste we generate. Marine debris includes timber, glass, metal and plastic from many different sources. Recently, the accumulation and possible impacts of microplastic particles in the ocean have been recognized as an emerging environmental issue. Some scientists are increasingly concerned about the potential impact of releases of persistent bio-accumulating and toxic compounds (PBTs) from plastic debris. At the same time, the fishing and tourism industries in many parts of the world are affected economically by plastic entering nets, fouling propellers and other equipment, and washing up on beaches. Despite international efforts to stem the flow of plastic debris, it continues to accumulate and impact the marine environment. To reduce the quantity of plastic entering the ocean, existing management instruments need to be made more effective and all aspects of waste treatment and disposal need to be improved.

Several common types of plastic are buoyant and have been transported by ocean currents to the remotest regions of the planet, including the Arctic and Antarctic (Barnes et al. 2010). Media attention has focused on reports of the relatively high incidence of plastic debris in areas of the ocean referred to as 'convergence zones' or 'ocean gyres'. This has given rise to the widespread use of terms like 'plastic soup', 'garbage patch' and 'ocean landfill'. Such terms are rather misleading in that much of the plastic debris in the ocean consists of fragments that are very small in size while the areas where they are floating are not, for example, distinguishable on satellite images. Nevertheless, publicity resulting from media reports and from the activities of several NGOs has helped to raise public and political awareness of the global scale of the plastic debris problem, together with the larger issue of marine litter.

Assessing the extent of the problem

It is difficult to quantify the amounts and sources of plastic and other types of debris entering the ocean. Land-based sources include poorly managed landfills, riverine transport, untreated sewage and storm water discharges, industrial and manufacturing facilities with inadequate controls, wind-blown debris, recreational use of coastal areas, and tourist activities (Barnes et al. 2009). These sources are thought to dominate the overall supply of marine debris, but there are important regional variations. For example, shipping and fisheries are significant contributors in the East Asian Seas region and the southern North Sea (UNEP/COBSEA 2009, Galgani et al. 2010). In general, more litter is found closer to population centres, including a greater proportion of consumer plastic items such as bottles, shopping bags and personal hygiene products (Ocean Conservancy 2010).

The greatest technological development of modern plastics occurred during the first half of the 20th century. Their production and use have continued to expand rapidly up to the present day (**Figure 1**). In many sectors, they have become a popular material for packaging (**Box 1**). A major benefit of their use in the food industry is that it can extend shelf life, thus decreasing the risk of infection and reducing food waste.

Ship- and platform-based sources of plastic litter in the ocean include fishing and recreational vessels, cruise liners, merchant shipping, oil and gas platforms, and aquaculture facilities (**Figure 2**).

Microplastics are generally considered to be plastic particles smaller than 5 millimetres in diameter (Arthur et al. 2009).

Persistent, bio-accumulating and toxic substances (PBTs) have a range of chronic health effects, including endocrine disruption, mutagenicity and carcinogenicity. A subset is regulated under the Stockholm Convention on Persistent Organic Pollutants (POPs).

Authors: Peter Kershaw (chair), Saido Katsuhiko, Sangjin Lee, Jon Samseth and Doug Woodring
Science writer: John Smith

Box 1: Consumer plastics—uses and fate

Most packaging and products in the waste stream are made of a small group of commodity plastics, including polyethylene (PE), polypropylene (PP), polyethylene terephthalate (PET), polyvinyl chloride (PVC), polystyrene (PS) and polyamide (PA), better known as nylon (Andrady and Neal 2009, PlasticsEurope 2010). These plastics have different properties, reflecting their intended uses. Their different properties may affect their durability and fate in the ocean. For example, PE and PP are less dense than seawater and will tend to be buoyant, whereas PS, PA and PET are denser and will tend to sink. All of these plastics can be recovered and recycled if there is appropriate infrastructure and willingness on the part of the public. Collecting and recycling mixed types of plastic remains a challenge, although separation based on density difference can be effective. Consumer plastic objects often find their way to the ocean through a combination of poor waste management practices, inadequate policies and regulation, ineffective enforcement, and the attitude and behaviour of individuals.

The major drivers of plastic use are improved physical or chemical properties compared with alternatives; low cost; mass production capability; and a reduction in the use of resources. Moreover, life-cycle analysis has shown that using plastic, rather than alternatives, often results in significant reductions in energy consumption and greenhouse gas emissions in applications ranging from food containers to vehicles and aircraft (PWC/Ecobilan 2004).

The applications of plastics in consumer products are many and varied. There are also significant regional differences in their use and disposal. Polyethylene bags are commonly used in West Africa to provide safe drinking water, but they often end up in water bodies due to a lack of waste disposal facilities. In Europe, approximately 38 per cent of plastics are used for disposable packaging (Barnes et al. 2009). Quantitative data for many countries are difficult to obtain, particularly on the use and fate of single-use items such as bottles, carrier bags and food packaging.

Use of plastic materials reached approximately 100 kg per year per capita in North America and Western Europe in 2005 and is expected to increase to 140 kg by 2015. Rapidly developing Asian countries constitute the world's largest potential growth area, with current use of around 20 kg plastic per year per person estimated to increase to 36 kg by 2015 (EuPC et al. 2009). Rates of plastic recycling and re-use vary greatly, even within developed regions. For example, in 2009 more than 84 per cent of used plastics were recovered—that is, recycled or reused for energy generation—in seven EU countries, as well as in Norway and Switzerland. Several European countries recovered only 25 per cent or less (EuPC et al. 2009, PlasticsEurope 2010). Improving waste management operations is an often overlooked opportunity for innovation and job creation, especially in many developing countries, where only a small percentage of the plastics produced are recovered.

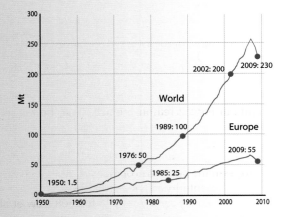

Figure 1: Growth in plastics production, 1950-2009. After five decades of continuous growth in world plastics production, there was a drop in production in 2008 due to the economic downturn. Close to 25 per cent of world production takes place in Europe. Plastics represented in the figure are thermoplastics, polyurethanes, thermosets, elastomers, adhesives, coatings and sealants, and polypropylene fibres. PET, PA and polyacryl fibres are not included. *Source: PlasticsEurope 2010*

There are large regional differences in the relative importance of these potential sources (GESAMP 2010). Discharges of plastic and other litter from ships and offshore structures are addressed under international law, but implementation and enforcement are often inadequate (NAS 2009, UNEP 2009a, Galgani et al. 2010).

Ocean circulation greatly affects the redistribution and accumulation of marine debris, as do the mass, buoyancy and persistence of the material (Moore et al. 2001). Computer model simulations, based on data from about 12 000 satellite-tracked floats deployed since the early 1990s as part of the Global Ocean Drifter Program (GODP 2011), confirm that debris will be subject to transport by ocean currents and will tend to accumulate in a limited number of sub-tropical convergence zones or gyres

A sample of plastic debris taken on board R.V. Meteor found at more than 4 200 metres water depth in the Ierapetra Basin south of Crete in Greece. *Credit: Michael Türkay, Senckenberg Research Institut Frankfurt, Germany*

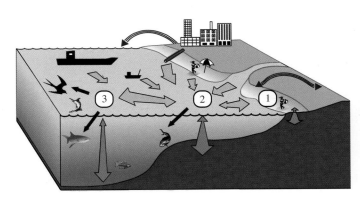

Figure 2: Main sources and movement pathways for plastic in the marine environment. Most plastic accumulates on beaches (1), in coastal waters and their sediments (2), and in the open ocean (3). Dark blue arrows depict wind-blown litter; grey arrows water-borne litter; orange arrows vertical movement through the water column, including burial in sediments; and black arrows ingestion by marine organisms. *Source: Adapted from Ryan et al. (2009)*

Attempting to stem the flow of plastic debris to the sea after heavy rain in southern California, the United States. *Credit: Bill Macdonald*

(IPRC 2008) (**Figure 3**). For this reason, the debris may be washed ashore on remote mid-ocean islands far from the source. The model simulations suggest that the debris may remain in the gyres for many years, but this does not take into account any other processes or changes in the properties of the particles.

A recent study presented data on plastic accumulation in the North Atlantic and Caribbean from 1986 to 2008 (Law et al. 2010). The highest concentrations (> 200 000 pieces per square kilometre) occurred in the convergence zones, as predicted by the model used, but there was no significant increase in concentration during this 22-year period. Although the authors speculate about possible causes, such as loss due to sinking or fragmentation to sizes not retained by the sampling net, they conclude that the results illustrate the current lack of knowledge of both sources and ocean sinks (Law et al. 2010). A proportion of the debris is thought to be ejected during the average of three years required for one revolution to be completed within the convergence zone (Ebbesmeyer and Sciglinao 2009). A study of microplastics in zooplankton samples from the Southern California Coastal Current again showed no significant change in the proportion of the microplastics during a 25-year span (Gilfillan et al. 2009). Inadequate waste management, combined with population growth and economic factors, could also affect plastic accumulation trends in other regions. However, there are no data available to confirm this yet.

For practical reasons, it is more difficult to monitor the accumulation of debris on the seabed than in the upper part of the water column. An extensive survey of the northwest European continental shelf revealed a widespread distribution of debris, mostly but not exclusively plastic (> 70 per cent), from varied sources (Galgani et al. 2000). Deep-water canyons appeared to be depositories for material from land-based sources. The quantity of fishing-related material was associated with known fishing activity. The Census of Marine Life programme, completed in 2010, reported finding plastic debris at abyssal depths. Such findings are not uncommon (Galil et al. 1995). Plastics at these depths will take much longer to fragment due to lack of ultraviolet (UV) penetration and much colder water temperatures.

Monitoring, surveillance and research focusing on plastic and other types of marine litter have increased in recent years. Nevertheless, a comprehensive set of environmental indicators for use in assessments has been lacking, as have related social and economic indicators. These types of indicators could include trends in coastal population increase and urbanization, plastics production, fractions of waste recycled, tourism revenue, waste disposal methods, shipping tonnage and fishing activities. Indicators also provide a means to measure the effectiveness of mitigation measures, such as improved waste management and the introduction of economic measures.

At the regional level, the European Commission is developing methods to assess the extent of the marine litter problem. This activity is taking place under the comprehensive Marine Strategy Framework Directive (EU 2008, Galgani et al. 2010), with indicators being produced to monitor progress towards achieving 'good environmental status' by 2020. The indicators cover the amount, distribution and composition of litter in four categories: washed

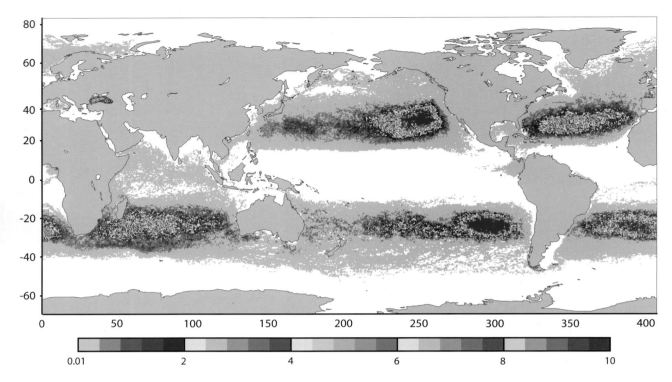

Figure 3: A model simulation of the distribution of marine litter in the ocean after ten years shows plastic converging in the five gyres: the Indian Ocean gyre, the North and South Pacific gyres, and the North and South Atlantic gyres. The simulation, derived from a uniform initial distribution and based on real drifter movements, shows the influence of the five main gyres over time. *Source: IPRC 2008*

Plastic ingested by a Laysan albatross in the Pacific. Knowing how and where marine organisms come into contact with marine debris could help in the design of management strategies to mitigate its environmental impacts. *Source: Young et al. (2009)*

ashore and/or disposed on coastlines; at sea and on the seabed; impacting marine animals; and microplastics (Galgani et al. 2010). This approach could furnish a useful example for other regional programmes with regard to producing indicators of ecological health, such as those related to the Ecological Quality Objective (EcoQO).

Routine offshore monitoring of plastic in the water column by traditional surveys tends to be costly and limited in geographical extent and frequency. This has led to an ongoing search for more cost-effective quantitative techniques. Measurements of plastic in the stomachs of stranded seabirds in the Northeast Atlantic have been used since 1977 to monitor sub-regional distributions and time trends, comparing the results with an EcoQO target (10 milligrams per bird). Fulmars, together with other species of offshore-feeding birds, such as petrels, auklets and albatrosses, are indiscriminate foragers and have been found to contain plastic objects in their guts that could be passed on to chicks (Ryan et al. 2009, Young et al. 2009). The highest levels of plastics in fulmars were found in the 1990s. Current levels are similar to those found

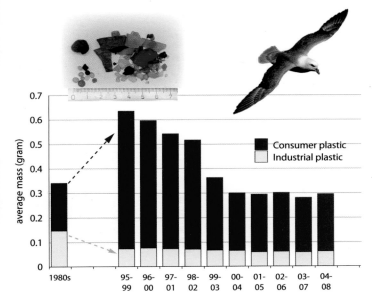

Figure 4: Consumer and industrial plastic ingested by beached fulmars in the North Sea, 1980s–2008. Since the 1980s the average mass of industrial plastic found has been halved. The intake of consumer plastic tripled in the mid-1990s, but has decreased since. *Source: van Franeker et al. (2010). Credit: Jan van Franeker, IMARES*

in the 1980s, but with no further reduction in quantity. The only change has been in composition, from industrial to consumer dominated plastics (van Franeker et al. 2010) (**Figure 4**). In a study using short-tailed shearwaters in the east Bering Sea, carried out between the 1970s and the late 1990s, Vlietstra and Parga (2002) reported a similar change in the source of plastics.

The EcoQO-related indicators provide a means of testing the effectiveness of mitigation measures. In Dutch waters, 90 per cent of litter washed ashore comes from merchant shipping or fishing (van Franeker et al. 2010). While implementation of EU legislation to improve port waste reception facilities began in the mid-2000s, no reduction in the amount of plastic in fulmar stomachs has occurred since, suggesting lack of compliance (van Franeker et al. 2010). Some additional indicators for marine debris have been developed, but they have not been widely applied.

Physical and chemical impacts

Environmental damage due to plastic and other marine debris can be defined as mortality or sub-lethal effects on biodiversity through physical damage by ingestion; entanglement in 'ghost nets' (fishing nets lost or left in the ocean) and other debris; chemical contamination by ingestion; and alteration of

community structure, including the importation of alien species (Galgani et al. 2010). Exposure of plastic debris to the variety of physical, chemical and biological processes in oceans results in fragmentation and size reduction (**Box 2**). In general, potential chemical effects are likely to increase with a reduction in the size of plastic particles while physical effects, such as the entanglement of seals and other animals in drift plastic, increase with the size and complexity of the debris.

More than 260 species are reported to have been entangled in, or to have ingested, marine debris (Laist 1997, Derraik 2002, Macfadyen et al. 2009). A recent study of planktivorous fish from the North Pacific gyre found an average of 2.1 plastic items per fish (Boerger et al. 2010). Ingestion of plastics mistaken for food is well documented in seabirds, sea turtles and marine mammals and can be fatal (Jacobsen et al. 2010). Albatrosses may mistake red plastic for squid, while sea turtles may mistake plastic bags for jellyfish. However, the extent to which ingestion of plastic has an impact on species at the level of populations is difficult to quantify, especially if there are additional pressures such as loss of breeding sites or over-exploitation. Ingested particles may cause an obstruction or otherwise damage the gut lining. Alternatively, these particles may result in poor nutrition through being substituted for food (Young et al. 2009), but such effects appear to be specific to certain species. Floating plastic objects or fragments also provide a temporary 'home' or vector for invasive species, including sessile invertebrates, seaweeds and pathogens (Astudillo et al. 2009).

Concerns about the potential chemical impacts of plastic in the ocean are two-fold: besides the potential impacts of releases of additives that were part of its original formulation, there are the

Fish farms off the Pacific coast of South America are an important source of plastic debris in the region. Detached buoys could be responsible for the dispersal of associated organisms in the Southeast Pacific. *Credit: Cristián Gutiérrez, Oceana*

Box 2: Plastic's slow degradability in the ocean

Plastic, like many other materials, is quickly fouled in seawater. These items retrieved from the ocean are covered with barnacles. *Credit: Algalita Marine Research Foundation*

The degradation time for plastic in the marine environment is, for the most part, unknown. Estimates are in the region of hundreds of years. Most types of plastic cannot be considered biodegradable in this environment, as the term 'biodegradable' would only apply to those that are broken down by bacterial action or oxidation into simpler molecules such as methane, carbon dioxide and water (Narayan 2009). 'Biodegradable' or 'oxy-degradable' plastics may be broken down in industrial composters, or in landfill, in a controlled environment with a temperature consistently above 58°C (Song et al. 2009). The temperature in most oceans is far below that, and the degradation process is therefore much slower.

Plastic in the ocean tends to fragment into smaller particles of similar composition, a process aided by the action of waves and wind. UV radiation in sunlight plays an important role in breaking down certain plastics (PP, PE). When plastic is manufactured, a UV stabilizing agent is sometimes added to extend the 'life' of certain items, also making it harder for them to break down after disposal. Seawater absorbs and scatters UV, so that plastics floating at or near the surface will break down more rapidly than those at depth. When plastic objects sink to the seabed, the breakdown process is slowed significantly since there is virtually no UV penetration and temperatures are much colder. Plastic debris has been observed on the ocean floor from the depths of the Fram Strait in the North Atlantic to deepwater canyons off the Mediterranean coast, and much of the plastic that has entered the North Sea is thought to reside on the seabed (Galgani et al. 1996, Galgani et al. 2000, Galgani and Lecornu 2004).

The surface of most plastic objects is subject to fouling in the sea due to the growth of bacteria, algae, barnacles, shellfish and other organisms. This process spans the entire size spectrum of debris, from microplastics to large single items such as buoys. A biological surface layer may affect breakdown mechanisms. Fouling may also increase the density of plastic objects, causing them to sink, with particles being redistributed throughout the whole water column and some eventually sinking to the ocean floor. Later removal of the biological surface layer by grazing organisms may cause the objects to float upwards.

potential impacts of releases of persistent, bio-accumulating and toxic substances (PBTs) that have accumulated in plastic particles over time.

The first concern relates to some of the compounds used in the manufacture of plastics, such as nonylphenol, phthalates, bisphenol A (BPA) and styrene monomers, as these can have adverse health effects at high concentrations. This may include impacts on the endocrine system involved in regulating hormone balance. Some studies have suggested that such effects might be expected on land and in freshwater ecosystems (Teuten et al. 2009). In contrast, an analysis of BPA monitoring data concluded that adverse effects would only occur to a very limited extent in highly industrialized areas (Klecka et al. 2009). The degree to which these compounds persist in the marine environment and

affect marine organisms is not well quantified by scientists, and further work is needed to assess the potential impact.

The second concern relates to the accumulation of PBTs in small plastic particles (**Box 3**). All kinds of plastic debris, from nets and other fishing gear to the thousands of different consumer items that find their way to the ocean, break down into fragments that can sorb PBTs that are already present in seawater and sediments (Mato et al. 2001, Rios et al. 2007, Macfadyen et al. 2009). PBTs include polychlorinated biphenols (PCBs), polyaromatic hydrocarbons (PAHs), hexachlorocyclohexane (HCH) and the insecticide DDT, together with other Persistent Organic Pollutants (POPs) that are covered under the Stockholm Convention (Stockholm Convention on Persistent Organic Pollutants 2011). Many of these pollutants, including PCBs, cause chronic effects

Box 3: Plastic pellets

Plastic resin pellets are small granules, generally in the shape of a cylinder or disc, with a diameter of a few millimetres. These particles are an industrial raw material that is remelted and moulded into final products. They enter the ocean as a result of spills or accidental releases. Like other plastic particles, they have been shown to accumulate PBTs. In the case of thin plastic films, for example those 50 micrometres or less, it may take only a few days for this process of accumulation or release to occur (Adams et al. 2007). In the case of pellets, equilibrium between the concentration of a given compound in a pellet and in the surrounding water or sediment may take many weeks or months. Older pellets consequently tend to have higher concentrations of contaminants and have been used to map the distribution of pollution in coastal waters around the world (Ogata et al. 2009, International Pellet Watch 2011) (**Figure 5**). Their consistent size makes them a useful monitoring tool.

Transport by plastic particles does not represent a significant additional flux of PBTs on a global scale compared with atmospheric or water transport (Zarfl and Matthies 2010). However, the concentration of contaminants by microplastic particles presents the possibility of increasing exposure to organisms through ingestion and entrance into the food chain—with the prospect of biomagnification in top-end predators in the food chain such as swordfish and seals. Ingestion of small particles by a wide variety of organisms has been well reported. However, the basic information needed on the biochemical and physiological response of organisms to ingested plastics contaminated with PBTs in order to quantify the scale of the problem is currently unavailable (Arthur et al. 2009, GESAMP 2010). It is conceivable that PBTs in plastic particles will be less bioavailable than those from the surrounding water or food sources (Gouin et al. 2011).

Collected from beaches around the world, plastic pellets like these have been found to accumulate persistent, bio-accumulating and toxic substances. The pellets are used in the manufacture of plastic products and have been introduced into the ocean through accidental releases. They may also be released as a result of poor handling or waste management. While there is evidence that quantities entering the marine environment have been reduced as a result of improved industrial practices, pellets already released will persist for many years. *Credit: International Pellet Watch*

Figure 5: Concentration of PCBs in beached plastic resin pellets, in nanograms per gram of pellet. Samples of polyethylene pellets have been collected at 56 beaches in 29 countries and analyzed for concentrations of organochlorine compounds. PCB concentrations were highest in pellets collected in the United States, Western Europe and Japan. They were lowest in those collected in tropical Asia and Africa. This spatial pattern reflects regional differences in the use of PCBs. *Source: Ogata et al. (2009) with additional data provided by International Pellet Watch in 2010*

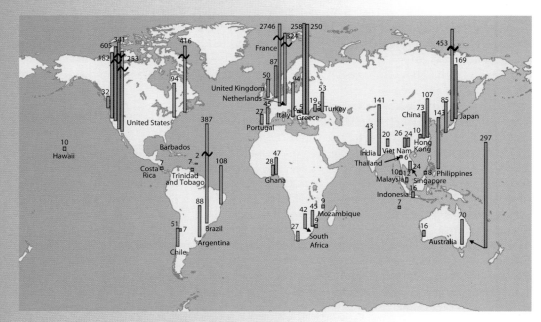

such as endocrine disruption affecting reproduction, increases in the frequency of genetic mutations (mutagenicity) and a tendency to cause cancer (carcinogenicity). Some scientists are concerned that these persistent contaminants could eventually end up in the food chain, although there is currently great uncertainty about the degree to which this poses a threat to human and ecosystem health (Arthur et al. 2009, Teuten et al. 2009, Thompson et al. 2009, GESAMP 2010).

We know that microplastics are ubiquitous in the ocean, contain a wide range of chemical contaminants, and can be ingested by marine organisms. However, the lack of certainty about the possible role of microplastics, as an additional vector for contaminants taken up by organisms, calls for caution and further research.

Social and economic effects: 'wider than the ocean'

Costs associated with the presence of plastic and other types of marine debris are often borne by those affected rather than those responsible for the problem (ten Brink et al. 2009, Mouat et al. 2010). The most obvious impacts are economic, such as loss of fishing opportunities due to time spent cleaning litter from nets, propellers and blocked water intakes. Marine litter costs the Scottish fishing industry an average of between US$15 million and US$17 million per year, the equivalent of 5 per cent of the total revenue of affected fisheries. Marine litter is also a significant ongoing navigational hazard for vessels, as reflected in the increasing number of coastguard rescues to vessels with fouled propellers in Norway and the United Kingdom: there were 286 such rescues in British waters in 2008, at a cost of up to US$2.8 million (Mouat et al. 2010).

Cleanups of beaches and waterways can be expensive. In the Netherlands and Belgium, approximately US$13.65 million per year is spent on removing beach litter. Cleanup costs for municipalities in the United Kingdom have increased by 38 per cent over the last ten years, to approximately US$23.62 million annually (Mouat et al. 2010). It is estimated that removing litter from South Africa's wastewater streams effectively would cost about US$279 million per year (ten Brink et al. 2009).

Other considerations include 'aesthetic intangible costs'. Litter can affect the public's perception of the quality of the surrounding environment. This, in turn, can lead to loss of income by local communities engaged in tourism, and in some cases by national economies dependent on tourism and associated economic activities (ten Brink et al. 2009, Mouat et al. 2010). Broken plastic, like broken glass, also has the potential to injure or greatly inconvenience beach users.

The Asia-Pacific Economic Cooperation (APEC) has reported that, in the Asia-Pacific region alone, marine debris is estimated to cost more than US$1 billion per year for activities ranging from cleanups to boat repairs. Fishing, transportation and tourism industries in many countries, as well as governments and local communities, suffer from the negative impacts of marine debris (McIlgorm et al. 2008, Ocean Conservancy 2010).

Tackling the issues, managing the problems

Despite the existence of a number of international conventions (**Box 4**), the problem of plastic and other marine debris in the ocean persists. This points to a lack of effective global, regional and national strategies to address municipal and other sources of waste. It also suggests deficiencies in the implementation and enforcement of existing regulations and standards, some of which may lack economic support.

A number of countries have taken steps at the national level to address this problem with legislation and the enforcement of regional and international agreements through national regulations. However, in many countries such initiatives either do not exist or are ineffective.

A wide variety of economic instruments can be used to help change attitudes and behaviour (ten Brink et al. 2009). To be successful, they need to be accompanied by concrete actions and effective implementation, underpinned by information, education, public awareness, capacity-building and technology transfer programmes. Examples include encouraging the development and use of appropriate reception facilities for ship-generated wastes, co-operative action within the fishing sector, consideration of life-cycles in product design to reduce plastic waste, and improvements in waste management practices.

The Global Programme of Action for the Protection of the Marine Environment from Land-based Activities

The Global Programme of Action (GPA) for the Protection of the Marine Environment from Land-based Activities, whose Secretariat is provided by UNEP, is the only global initiative that directly addresses the link between watersheds, coastal waters and the open ocean (UNEP/GPA 2011). It provides a mechanism for the development and implementation of initiatives to tackle transboundary issues. Plastic and other types of marine debris are such an issue. To help improve the knowledge base, UNEP has collaborated with the Intergovernmental Oceanographic Commission of the United Nations Educational, Scientific and Cultural Organization (UNESCO-IOC) to develop Guidelines on

Box 4: International conventions

The issue of marine debris has been addressed by the United Nations General Assembly within the context of its annual resolutions on oceans and the law of the sea and on sustainable fisheries. In 2005, this issue was also considered as a topic of focus of the sixth meeting of the United Nations Open-ended Informal Consultative Process on Oceans and the Law of the Sea. Two major international conventions specifically address marine litter in the ocean: the International Convention for the Prevention of Pollution from Ships, 1973, as modified by the Protocol of 1978 (MARPOL 73/78); and the Convention on the Prevention of Marine Pollution by Dumping of Wastes and Other Matter 1972 (commonly referred to as the London Convention) with its 1996 Protocol (the London Protocol). However, despite restrictions on disposal of waste based on its type and the distance from land, and a complete ban on the disposal of plastics at sea, the world's beaches and oceans continue to be polluted by plastic and other types of marine debris. The coverage of these conventions in general is considered to be adequate, but their implementation and enforcement may need to be strengthened (NAS 2009).

The purpose of MARPOL 73/78 is to control pollution from shipping by regulating the types and quantities of waste that ships discharge to the marine environment. MARPOL Annex V on the prevention of pollution by garbage from ships has been in force since 1988. Under Annex V, 'garbage' includes all types of food, domestic and operational waste, excluding fresh fish, generated during normal operation of the vessel and liable to be disposed of continuously or periodically. Disposal of plastics into the sea anywhere is strictly forbidden. Annex V also obliges governments to ensure the provision of reception facilities at ports and terminals for the reception of garbage. The International Maritime Organization (IMO) has actively encouraged countries to improve these facilities. Annex V has been under review by the IMO, and amendments to revise and update it are to be considered for adoption in July 2011 (IMO 2011).

The London Convention covers the control of dumping of wastes at sea that have been generated on land. It requires the signatories (86 states) to prohibit dumping of persistent plastics and other non-biodegradable

materials, as well as certain compounds, into the sea. In addition, the 1982 United Nations Convention on the Law of the Sea (UNCLOS) sets out the legal framework within which all activities in the oceans and seas must be carried out. Part XII (Articles 192-237), in particular, concerns the Protection and Preservation of the Marine Environment. It sets out general obligations to prevent, reduce and control pollution from land-based sources, including rivers, estuaries, pipelines and outfall structures; from seabed activities subject to national jurisdiction; from activities in a designated Area, that is, the seabed, ocean floor and subsoil thereof, beyond the limits of national jurisdiction; from vessels; by dumping; and from or through the atmosphere.

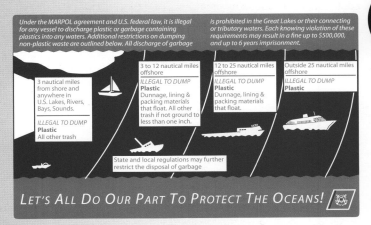

Vessels in the United States are required to maintain garbage record books and shipboard management plans and to display placards such as this one, notifying crew and passengers of the requirements of MARPOL Annex V. A violation may result in a fine or imprisonment. *Credit: United States Coast Guard, reproduced in NAS (2009)*

---

the Survey and Monitoring of Marine Litter (Cheshire et al. 2009). In collaboration with the Food and Agriculture Organization of the United Nations (FAO), a comprehensive report on abandoned, lost or otherwise discarded fishing gear has been published (Macfadyen et al. 2009).

Regional initiatives

Regional co-operation is essential if the problem of plastic debris in the ocean is to be addressed successfully. The Global Initiative on Marine Litter, a co-operative activity of UNEP/GPA and the UNEP Regional Seas Programme (UNEP/RSP), has organized and implemented numerous regional marine litter activities. Regional Seas programmes involved comprise Black Sea, Wider

Caribbean, East Asian Seas, Eastern Africa, South Asian Seas, ROPME Sea Area, Mediterranean, North-East Pacific, North-West Pacific, Red Sea and Gulf of Aden, South-East Pacific, Pacific, and Western Africa. Activities have included collaboration with the Ocean Conservancy's International Coastal Cleanup (ICC) to raise awareness of the marine debris issue in regions and to encourage greater public education and engagement. The 18 Regional Seas Conventions and Action Plans could serve as platforms for developing common regional strategies and promoting synergies, mainly at the national level, to prevent, reduce and remove marine litter (UNEP 2009b).

Providing incentives for portside disposal of ship-generated waste is one practical means of curbing waste discharges at sea. In addition, providing economic incentives to dispose of waste

Measures to reduce the amount of marine litter entering the ocean can be made more effective by providing ports with adequate and inexpensive reception facilities for disposal of vessel garbage, such as this container at the port of Bristol, United Kingdom. *Credit: Bristol Port Company*

onshore can prevent illegal discharges. An example is the no-special-fee system for oils and waste discharged to port reception facilities in the Baltic Sea Area (HELCOM 2011).

National and local initiatives

Ways to better understand and ultimately reduce the flow of plastic debris to the ocean are being sought through a range of national and local initiatives. For example, in the United States improved monitoring and assessment methods have been developed to identify and quantify the amounts and composition of marine litter. This initiative is co-ordinated by the National Oceanic and Atmospheric Administration (NOAA) and its partners. In the United Kingdom, the Waste and Resources Action Programme (WRAP) encourages businesses to reduce waste, increase recycling and decrease reliance on landfill (WRAP 2011). To help raise awareness, UNEP and NOAA are co-hosting the 5th International Marine Debris Conference in March 2011 (IMDC 2011).

Industry initiatives

The problem of plastic debris in the ocean has been recognized by a number of industry sectors. For example, regional Marine Environment Protection Associations (MEPAs) have been established by the shipping sector to preserve the marine environment through educating those in the sector, port communities and children. This initiative was started in Greece in 1982 by the local shipping community as a response to public

concern about marine pollution in the Mediterranean (HELMEPA 2011). Several regional initiatives followed. They are now co-ordinated by the International Marine Environment Protection Association (INTERMEPA). The MEPAs' commitment 'To Save the Seas' includes voluntary co-operation to protect the marine environment from pollution, awareness and educational activities, promotion of health and safety standards, and enhancement of quality standards and professional competence throughout the organization's membership (INTERMEPA 2011).

The American and British plastics industries have implemented Operation Clean Sweep to reduce losses of resin pellets to the environment, particularly during their transport and shipment. Motivated by the need to comply with legislation, but also sound economics and good environmental stewardship, Operation Clean Sweep is contributing to the reduction of plastic pellets found in marine debris (Operation Clean Sweep 2011).

The Fishing for Litter campaign is an example of a low-cost voluntary activity. Developed through the Local Authorities International Environmental Organisation, it encourages fishers based around the North Sea to collect and bring to port any litter retrieved in their nets (KIMO 2011). This approach, promoted through co-operation between the industry and local government, was adopted by the OSPAR Commission under the Convention for the Protection of the Marine Environment of the North-East Atlantic in 2007. An alternative approach to reduce marine litter in the Republic of Korea has been through the Waste Fishing Gear Buy-back Project (Macfadyen et al. 2009). In South East Asia, the Green Fins project is an initiative by the diving tourism industry that promotes sustainable use of coral reefs. It includes clearing discarded fishing nets and other debris from reefs (Green Fins 2011).

NGO initiatives

Several NGOs are focusing on plastic debris in the ocean. The Algalita Marine Research Foundation has been prominent since 1997 in conducting ocean surveys and promoting research projects, initially in the North Pacific and extending into the North Atlantic and Indian Oceans (Algalita 2011). It is one of a number of NGOs that supports the 5 Gyres initiative, which is currently investigating the distribution of microplastics and POPs in each of the five main ocean gyres in conjunction with Pangea Expeditions and the UN Safe Planet Campaign (5 Gyres 2011). Another novel initiative is the Travel Trawl. Using equipment loaned to them, citizen scientists collect samples of plastic debris during their own sailing voyages and report their findings to the Algalita Foundation (Travel Trawl 2011).

In 2009, Project Kaisei collaborated with the Scripps Institution of Oceanography to support a graduate student-led expedition to explore and analyze plastic debris in the North Pacific gyre (Scripps Institution 2009). Project Kaisei is testing ways to remove some of the plastic in the ocean using low-energy catch methods. Further studies are designed to determine types of remediation or recycling that could be applied to collected plastic material, including derelict fishing nets, so that there will be some potential for economic value creation to subsidize cleanup efforts (Project Kaisei 2011).

The annual International Coastal Cleanup organized by the Ocean Conservancy is the world's largest volunteer effort to collect information on the amounts and types of marine debris. In 2009, 498 818 volunteers from 108 countries and locations collected 3 357 tonnes of debris from over 6 000 sites (Ocean Conservancy 2010) (**Figure 6**). Plastic bags, the second most common item removed, have much greater potential impact than the number one item (cigarettes/cigarette filters). Clean Up the

Raising awareness and bridging the gap between science and policy making. Debate on plastic in the ocean as part of the Royal Geographical Society (with IBG) 21st Century Challenges discussion series in London, the United Kingdom. Panelists included an oceanographer, a representative of the plastic industry and the skipper of the *Plastiki*. *Credit: Royal Geographical Society*

Rank	Debris item	Number
1	Cigarettes / cigarette filters	2 189 252
2	Bags (plastic)	1 126 774
3	Food wrappers / containers	943 233
4	Caps, lids	912 246
5	Beverage bottles (plastic)	883 737
6	Cups, plates, forks, knives, spoons	512 517
7	Beverage bottles (glass)	459 531
8	Beverage cans	457 631
9	Straws, stirrers	412 940
10	Bags (paper)	331 476
	Top 10 total debris items	8 229 337

Figure 6: Top ten marine debris items removed from the global coastline and waterways during the 2009 International Coastal Cleanup. The list shows that plastic is part of the overall marine litter problem, but it does not include some less common and potentially more hazardous plastic items such as discarded fishing nets. *Source: Ocean Conservancy*

World is another initiative started by an individual motivated to take action by the amount of plastic debris he discovered when sailing in the open ocean. Since 1993, it has developed into an international programme designed to encourage communities to work together to make a positive difference to the environment (CUW 2011).

In 2010 the *Plastiki*, a 60-foot catamaran made of 12 500 reclaimed plastic bottles and other recycled PET plastic and waste products, sailed from San Francisco to Sydney, Australia, to raise awareness of plastic in the ocean (Plastiki 2011). The voyage of the *Plastiki* took place two years after a 5 Gyres/Algalita project during which the *Junkraft*, made of 15 000 reclaimed plastic bottles, sailed through the North Pacific gyre (Junkraft 2008).

Looking ahead

More information is clearly required about the sources, distribution, fate and potential impact of plastics in the marine environment. This is particularly true in the case of microplastics, as we lack adequate knowledge of their potential physical and chemical effects on marine organisms. Information is needed at local, regional and global scales, as sources, circumstances, capabilities and mitigation strategies at each scale will vary. Solutions need to be part of comprehensive programmes to improve waste management generally: that is, waste collection and disposal infrastructure, waste management practices, and enforcement. Such programmes could include improved design and application of single-use plastics, increased consumer awareness and behavioural changes, improved recycling and re-use, and the introduction of economic instruments to reduce littering and promote secondary uses of plastic debris (ten Brink et al. 2009). Innovative technologies in the recycling sector present possibilities to recycle a greater proportion of waste and should be encouraged. Part of the answer may lie in the application of the concept of extended producer responsibility, according to which a producer's responsibility for a product is extended to the post-consumer stage of the product's life cycle (OECD 2006).

If plastic is treated as a valuable resource, rather than just as a waste product, any opportunities to create a secondary value for the material after its first intended use will provide economic incentives for collection and reprocessing. For example, in several European countries a large proportion of waste is used for energy generation in modern high-temperature furnaces, with strict emissions control. New technologies for turning plastic into diesel and other fuels could be a promising option for reducing the amounts of many types of plastic that are unlikely to be recycled, as well as new waste management revenue streams for communities and municipalities. However, it should be recognized that some smaller countries, particularly small island developing states (SIDS), have specific problems attracting investment and developing the appropriate infrastructure to deal with waste generated, for example, by the tourism industry.

Successful management of the global marine litter problem will require the development and implementation of effective policies and measures, supported by international and regional treaties and conventions—with decision-makers giving marine litter a higher profile in national environmental protection regulations and development plans. It will be especially important to use education and outreach programmes to encourage key user groups, industry sectors and the general public to modify behaviour and assume greater personal responsibility for their actions. Key user groups include individual fishers and their associations, sailors, tourists, consumer groups, sporting bodies, cruise operators and hoteliers. Tackling the plastic waste issue will demand political commitment, investment and an integrated approach at all levels of society, in order to prevent litter from reaching the ocean from sea- and land-based sources and to move towards a cleaner ocean, reducing the many pressures and impacts on biodiversity and, at the same time, greatly reducing related social and economic costs.

References

5 Gyres (2011). Understanding Plastic Pollution through Exploration, Education and Action. http://5gyres.org

Adams, R.G., Lohmann, R., Fernandez, L.A., MacFarlane, J.K. and Gschwend, P.M. (2007). Polyethylene Devices: Passive Samplers for Measuring Dissolved Hydrophobic Organic Compounds in Aquatic Environments. *Environmental Science and Technology*, 41(4), 1317-1323

Algalita (2011). Algalita Marine Research Foundation. http://www.algalita.org

Andrady, A.L. and Neal, M.A. (2009). Applications and societal benefits of plastics. *Philosophical Transactions of the Royal Society B: Biological Sciences*, 364(1526), 1977-1984

Arthur, C., Baker, J. and Bamford, H. (eds.) (2009). *Proceedings of the International Research Workshop on the Occurrence, Effects, and Fate of Microplastic Marine Debris, September 9-11, 2008*. National Oceanic and Atmospheric Administration Technical Memorandum NOS-OR&R-30

Astudillo, J.C., Bravo, M., Dumont, C.P. and Thiel, M. (2009). Detached aquaculture buoys in the SE Pacific: potential dispersal vehicles for associated organisms. *Aquatic Biology*, 5, 219-231

Barnes, D.K., Galgani, F., Thompson, R.C. and Barlaz, M. (2009). Accumulation and fragmentation of plastic debris in global environments. *Philosophical Transactions of the Royal Society B: Biological Sciences*, 364(1526), 1995-1998

Barnes, D.K.A., Walters, A. and Gonçalves, L. (2010). Macroplastics at sea around Antarctica. *Marine Environmental Research*, 70(2), 250-252

Boerger, C.M., Lattin, G.L., Moore, S.L. and Moore, C.J. (2010). Plastic ingestion by planktivorous fishes in the North Pacific Central Gyre. *Marine Pollution Bulletin*, 60(12), 2275-2278

Brink, P. ten, Lutchman, I., Bassi, S., Speck, S., Sheavly, S., Register, K. and Woolaway, C. (2009). *Guidelines on the Use of Market-based Instruments to Address the Problem of Marine Litter*. Institute for European Environmental Policy (IEEP), Brussels, Belgium, and Sheavly Consultants, Virginia Beach, USA

Cheshire, A.C., Adler, E., Barbière, J., Cohen, Y., Evans, S., Jarayabhand, S., Jeftic, L., Jung, R.T., Kinsey, S., Kusui, E.T., Lavine, I., Manyara, P., Oosterbaan, L., Pereira, M.A., Sheavly, S., Tkalin, A., Varadarajan, S., Wenneker, B. and Westphalen, G. (2009). *UNEP/IOC Guidelines on Survey and Monitoring of Marine Litter*. UNEP Regional Seas Reports and Studies, No. 186; IOC Technical Series No. 83

CUW (2011). Clean Up the World. http://www.cleanuptheworld.org

Derraik, J.G.B. (2002) The pollution of the marine environment by plastic debris: a review. *Marine Pollution Bulletin*, 44, 842-852

Ebbesmeyer, C. and Scigliano, E. (2009). *Flotsametrics and the Floating World. How One Man's Obsession With Runaway Sneakers and Rubber Ducks Revolutionized Ocean Science*. Smithsonian Books/Collins/HarperCollins, Washington, D.C.

EU (European Union) (2008). Directive 2008/56/EC of the European Parliament and of the Council of 17 June 2008 establishing a framework for community action in the field of marine environmental policy (Marine Strategy Framework Directive)

EuPC (European Plastics Converters), EPRO (European Association of Plastics Recycling and Recovery Organisations), EuPR (European Plastics Recyclers) and PlasticsEurope (2009). *The Compelling Facts About Plastics 2009: An analysis of European plastics productivity, demand and recovery for 2008*

Franeker, J.A. van, Meijboom, A., de Jong, M. and Verdaat, H. (2010). *Fulmar litter EcoQO monitoring in the Netherlands 1979-2007 in relation to EU Directive 200/59/EC on Port Reception Facilities*. Report nr: C032/09. IMARES Wageningen UR.

Galgani, F., Fleet, D., van Franeker, J., Katsanevakis, S., Maes, T., Mouat, J., Oosterbaan, L., Poitou, I. Hanke, G., Thompson, R., Amato, E., Birkun, A. and Janssen, C. (2010). *Marine Strategy Framework Directive Task Team 10 Report Marine Litter*. JRC (EC Joint Research Centre) Scientific and Technical Reports

Galgani, F., Léauté, J.P., Moguedet, P., Souplet, A., Verin, Y., Carptentier, A., Goraguer, H., Latrouite, D., Andreal, B., Cadiou, Y., Mahe, J.C., Poulard, J.C. and Nerisson, P. (2000). Litter on the Sea Floor Along European Coasts. *Marine Pollution Bulletin*, 40(6), 516-527

Galgani, F. and Lecornu, F. (2004). Debris on the sea floor at 'Hausgarten': in the expedition ARKTIS XIX/3 of the research vessel POLARSTERN in 2003. *Berichte Polar Meeresforsch*, 488, 260-262

Galgani, F., Souplet, A. and Cadiou, Y. (1996). Accumulation of debris on the deep sea floor off the French Mediterranean coast. *Marine Ecology Progress Series*, 142(1-3), 225-234

Galil, B.S., Golik, A. and Türkay, M. (1995). Litter at the Bottom of the Sea: A Sea Bed Survey in the Eastern Mediterranean. *Marine Pollution Bulletin*, 30(1), 22-24.

GESAMP (2010), IMO/FAO/UNESCO-IOC/UNIDO/WMO/IAEA/UN/UNEP Joint Group of Experts on the Scientific Aspects of Marine Environmental Protection); Bowmer, T. and Kershaw, P.J., 2010 (eds.), *Proceedings of the GESAMP International Workshop on plastic particles as a vector in transporting persistent, bio-accumulating and toxic substances in the oceans*. GESAMP Reports and Studies No. 82

Gilfillan, L.R., Doyle, M.J., Ohman, M.D. and Watson, W. (2009). Occurrence of Plastic Micro-debris in the Southern California Current System. California Cooperative Oceanic Fisheries Investigations, *CalCOFI Rep*. 50

GODP (Global Ocean Drifter Program) (2011) The Global Ocean Drifter Program. Satellite-tracked surface drifting buoys. http://www.aoml.noaa.gov/phod/dac/gdp

Gouin, T., Roche, N., Lohmann, R., Hodges, G. (2011). A thermodynamic approach for assessing the environmental exposure of chemicals absorbed to microplastic. Environmental Science and Technology

Green Fins (2011). Green Fins Project is Underway in Indonesia, Malaysia, Philippines and Thailand. http://www.greenfins.net

HELCOM (2011). Application of the "No-Special-Fee" System in the Baltic Sea Area. Convention on the Protection of the Marine Environment of the Baltic Sea Area (Helsinki Commission). http://www.helcom.fi/Recommendations/en_GB/rec19_8/

HELMEPA (Hellenic Marine Environment Protection Association) (2011). 25 years of International Voluntary Action for Clean Beaches. http://www.helmepa.gr/en/index.php

IMDC (International Marine Debris Conference) (2011). Fifth International Marine Debris Conference. Waves of Change: Global lessons to inspire local action. http://www.5imdc.org

IMO (International Maritime Organization) (2011). Prevention of Pollution by Garbage from Ships. Regulations for the Prevention of pollution by garbage from ships are contained in Annex V of MARPOL. Overview of Annex V. http://www.imo.org/OurWork/Environment/PollutionPrevention/Garbage/Pages/Default.aspx

INTERMEPA (2011). International Marine Environment Protection Association. http://www.intermepa.org/about_us.html

International Pellet Watch (2011). Global Monitoring of Persistent Organic Pollutants (POPs) using Beached Plastic Resin Pellets. http://www.tuat.ac.jp/~gaia/ipw/

IPRC (International Pacific Research Center) (2008). Tracking Ocean Debris. *IPRC Climate*, 8, 2.

Jacobsen, J.K., Massey, L. and Gulland, F. (2010). Fatal ingestion of floating net debris by two sperm whales (*Physeter macrocephalus*). *Marine Pollution Bulletin*, 60(15), 765-767

Junkraft (2008). JUNK. Sailing to Hawaii on 15,000 Plastic Bottles and a Cessna 310 to Raise Awareness About Plastic Fouling Our Ocean. http://junkraft.blogspot.com

KIMO (Kommunenes Internasjonale Miljøorganisasjon/Local Authorities International Environmental Organisation) (2011). http://www.kimointernational.org

Klecka, G.M., Staples, C.A., Clark, K.E., van der Hoeven, N., Thomas, D.E., Hentges, S.G. (2009). Exposure analysis of bisphenol A in surface water systems in North America and Europe. *Environmental Science and Technology*, 43(16), 6145-6150

Laist, D.W. (1997). Impacts of marine debris: entanglement of marine life in marine debris including a comprehensive list of species with entanglement and ingestion records. In: *Marine debris: sources, impacts and solutions* (Coe, J.M. and Rogers, B.D., eds.), 99-141. Springer, Berlin.

Law, K.L., Morét-Ferguson, S., Maximenko, N.A., Proskurowski, G., Peacock, E.E., Hafner, J. and Reddy, C.M. (2010). Plastic Accumulation in the North Atlantic Subtropical Gyre. *Science*, 329 (5996), 1185-1188

Macfadyen, G., Huntington, T. and Cappell, R. (2009). *Abandoned, lost or otherwise discarded fishing gear*. UNEP Regional Seas Reports and Studies 185, FAO Fisheries and Aquaulture Technical Paper 523

Mato, Y., Isobe, T., Takada, H., Kanehiro, H., Ohtake, C. and Kaminuma, T. (2001). Plastic Resin Pellets as a Transport Medium for Toxic Chemicals in the Marine Environment. *Environmental Science and Technology*, 35(3), 318-324

McIlgorm, A., Campbell, H.F. and Rule, M.J. (2008). *Understanding the economic benefits and costs of controlling marine debris in the APEC region (MRC 02/2007). A report to the Asia-Pacific Economic Cooperation Marine Resource Conservation Working Group by the National Marine Science Centre (University of New England and Southern Cross University), Coffs Harbour, NSW, Australia, December*

Moore, C.J., Moore, S.L., Leecaster, M.K. and Weisberg, S.B. (2001). A comparison of plastic and plankton in the North Pacific Central Gyre. *Marine Pollution Bulletin*, 42(12), 1297-1300

Mouat, T., Lopez Lozano, R. and Bateson, H. (2010). *Economic Impacts of Marine Litter*. KIMO (Kommunenes Internasjonale Miljøorganisasjon/Local Authorities International Environmental Organisation

Narayan, R. (2009). Fundamental Principles and Concepts of Biodegradability – Sorting through the facts, hypes, and claims of biodegradable plastics in the marketplace. *bioplastics MAGAZINE*, 4, 01/09

NAS (National Academy of Sciences) (2009). *Tackling Marine Debris in the 21st Century*. National Research Council, Committee on the Effectiveness of International and National Measures to Prevent and Reduce Marine Debris and Its Impacts, Washington, D.C.

Ocean Conservancy (2010). Trash Travels. From Our Hands to the Sea, Around the Globe, and Through Time. http://www.oceanconservancy.org/images/2010ICCReportRelease_pressPhotos/2010_ICC_Report.pdf

OECD (Organisation for Economic Co-operation and Development) (2006). Fact Sheet: Extended Producer Responsibility. http://www.oecd.org/search/Result/0,3400,en_2649_201185_1_1_1_1_1,00.html

Ogata, Y., Takada, H., Mizukawa, K., Hirai, H., Iwasa, S., Endo, S., Mato, Y., Saha, M., Okuda, K., Nakashima, A., Murakami, M., Zurcher, N., Booyatumanondo, R., Zakaria, M.P., Dung, le Q, Gordon, M., Miguez, C., Suzuki, S., Moore, C., Karapanagioti, H.K., Weerts, S., McClurg, T., Burres, E., Smith, W., Van Velkenburg, M., Lang, J.S., Lang, R.C., Laursen, D., Danner, B., Stewardson, N., Thompson, R.C. (2009). International Pellet Watch: Global monitoring of persistent organic pollutants (POPs) in coastal waters 1. Initial phase data on PCBs, DDTS, and HCHs. *Marine Pollution Bulletin*, 58 (10), 1437-1446

Operation Clean Sweep (2011). Pellet Handling Manual. APC (American Plastics Council) and SPI (The Society of the Plastics Industry). http://www.opcleansweep.org/manual/OCSmanual

PlasticsEurope (2010). Plastics – the facts. http://www.plasticseurope.org

Plastiki (2011). Plastiki Time. Discover More About the Plastiki, A Boat Made of 12,000 Plastic Bottles. http://www.theplastiki.com

Project Kaisei (2011). Capturing the Plastic Vortex. http://www.projectkaisei.org

PWC/Ecobilan (2004). *Évaluation des impacts environnementaux des sacs de caisse Carrefour*. Price-Waterhouse-Coopers/Ecobilan. http://www.ademe.fr/htdocs/actualite/rapport_carrefour_post_revue_critique_v4.pdf

Rios, L.M., Moore, C. and Jones, P.R. (2007). Persistent organic pollutants carried by synthetic polymers in the ocean environment. *Marine Pollution Bulletin*, 54, 1230-1237

Ryan, P.G., Moore, C.J., van Franeker, J.A. and Moloney, C.L. (2009). Monitoring the abundance of plastic debris in the marine environment. *Philosophical Transactions of the Royal Society B: Biological Sciences*, 364(1526), 1999-2012

Scripps Institution (2009). SEAPLEX: Scripps Research Cruise, 17 August 2009. http://scrippsnews.ucsd.edu/Releases/?releaseID=1015

Song, J.H., Murphy, R.J., Narayan, R. and Davies, G.B.H. (2009). Biodegradable and compostable alternatives to conventional plastics. *Philosophical Transactions of the Royal Society B: Biological Sciences*, 364(1526), 2127-2139.

Stockholm Convention on Organic Pollutants (2011). What are POPs? http://www.pops.int

Teuten, E.L., Saqing, J.M., Knappe, D.R.U., Barlaz, M.A., Jonsson, S., Björn, A., Rowland, S.J., Thompson, R.C., Galloway, T.S., Yamashita, R., Ochi, D., Watanuki, Y., Moore, C., Viet, P.H., Tana, T.S., Prudente, M., Boonyatumanond, R., Zakaria, M.P., Akkhavong, K., Ogata, Y., Hirai, H., Iwasa, S., Mizukawa, K., Hagino, Y., Imamura, A., Saha, M. and Takada, H. (2009). Transport and release of chemicals from plastics to the environment and to wildlife. *Philosophical Transactions of the Royal Society B: Biological Sciences*, 364(1526), 2027-2045

Thompson, R.C., Moore, C.J., vom Saal, F.S. and Swan, S.H. (2009). Plastics, the environment and human health: current consensus and future trends. *Philosophical Transactions of the Royal Society B: Biological Sciences*, 364(1526), 2153-2166

Travel Trawl (2011). 5 Gyres: Our Travel Trawl Program. http://5gyres.org/get_involved/travel_trawl

UNEP (2009a). *Marine Litter: A Global Challenge*. United Nations Environment Programme

UNEP (2009b). UNEP's Global Initiative on Marine Litter. United Nations Environment Programme. http://www.unep.org/regionalseas/marinelitter/publications/docs/Marinelitter_Flyer2009.pdf

UNEP/COBSEA (2009). *State of the Marine Environment Report for the East Asian Seas 2009* (Chou , L.M. ed). COBSEA Secretariat, Bangkok.

UNEP/GPA (2011). Global Programme of Action for the Protection of the Marine Environment from Land-based Activities. http://www.gpa.unep.org/

Vlietstra, L.S. and Parga, J.A. (2002). Long-term changes in the type, but not amount, of ingested plastic particles in short-tailed shearwaters in the southeastern Bering Sea. *Marine Pollution Bulletin*, 44(9), 945-955

Young, L.C., Vanderlip, C., Duffy, D.C., Afanasyev, V. and Shaffer, S.A. (2009), Bringing Home the Trash: Do Colony-Based Differences in Foraging Distribution Lead to Increased Plastic Ingestion in Laysan Albatrosses? *PloS ONE*, 4, 10.

WRAP (Waste & Resource Action Programme) (2011). WRAP: Material change for a better environment. http://www.wrap.org.uk

Zarfl, C. and Matthies, M. (2010). Are marine plastic particles transport vectors for organic pollutants to the Arctic? *Marine Pollution Bulletin*, 60(10), 1810-1840

Until it was treated with phosphorus fertilizers, soil in Brazil's Cerrado region was largely agriculturally unproductive. Maize plants grown on phosphorus-treated soil are much taller than control plants like those in the foreground, which did not receive adequate additional phosphorus. *Credit: D.M.G. de Sousa*

Phosphorus and Food Production

Phosphorus is essential for food production, but its global supply is limited. Better insight is needed into the availability of this non-renewable resource and the environmental consequences associated with its use. Optimizing agricultural practices while exploring innovative approaches to sustainable use can reduce environmental pressures and enhance the long-term supply of this important plant nutrient.

Virtually every living cell requires phosphorus, the 11th most abundant element in the Earth's crust. However, the soil from which plants obtain phosphorus typically contains only small amounts of it in a readily available form. There is no known substitute for phosphorus in agriculture. If soils are deficient in phosphorus, food production is restricted unless this nutrient is added in the form of fertilizer. Hence, to increase the yield of plants grown for food, an adequate supply of phosphorus is essential.

Farming practices that are helping to feed billions of people include the application of phosphorus fertilizers manufactured from phosphate rock, a non-renewable resource used increasingly since the end of the 19th century. The dependence of food production on phosphate rock calls for sustainable management practices to ensure its economic viability and availability to farmers. While there are commercially exploitable amounts of phosphate rock in several countries, those with no domestic reserves could be particularly vulnerable in the case of global shortfalls.

Use of phosphorus in agriculture is associated with several types of potential environmental impacts. Too little phosphorus restricts plant growth, leading to soil erosion. Phosphorus overuse can result in losses to surface waters and eutrophication. More sustainable practices—such as better managed field applications and enhanced phosphorus recycling—can contribute to improvements in productivity and reduce environmental impacts while increasing the life-span of this finite resource. **Figure 1** shows the phosphorus flows in the environment. Although much is known about how to locally enhance soil fertility by adding phosphorus, there is a need for a more comprehensive understanding and better quantification of the global pathways.

Scientists are starting to quantify global phosphorus flows through the food production and consumption system. It is estimated that only one-fifth of the phosporus mined in the world is consumed by humans as food (Schröder et al. 2010). Yet important knowledge gaps remain concerning how much phosphorus is obtained, how much is used in agriculture and retained in soil, and how much is released to the aquatic environment or lost in food waste.

Supplying a critical nutrient

High crop yields today depend fundamentally on mined phosphate rock, a significant departure from historical food production methods. When the world population was much smaller, farmers could obtain adequate yields by fertilizing soil with phosphorus derived from human and animal excreta. Population growth in the 18th and 19th centuries stimulated food production, resulting in more rapid depletion of soil nutrients. Farmers therefore began to use increasing amounts of off-farm sources of phosphorus, including bone meal, guano and phosphate rock (Jacob 1964). Phosphate rock, which was cheap and plentiful, became the source that was widely preferred

---

Phosphorus resources and reserves

Resources are concentrations of naturally occurring phosphate material in such a form or amount that economic extraction of a product is currently or potentially feasible.

Reserves are the part of an identified resource that meets minimum criteria related to current mining and production practices, including grade, quality, thickness and depth, and that can be economically extracted or produced at the time of the determination. Use of this term does not signify that the necessary extraction facilities are in place or working.

Source: Adapted from Van Kauwenbergh (2010) and Jasinski (2011)

Authors: Keith Syers (chair), Mateete Bekunda, Dana Cordell, Jessica Corman, Johnny Johnston, Arno Rosemarin and Ignacio Salcedo
Science writer: Tim Lougheed

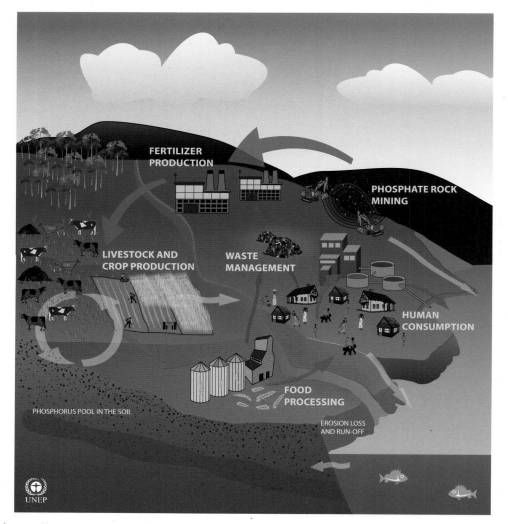

Figure 1: Phosphorus flows in the environment. To enhance food production, phosphorus is added to soil in the form of mineral fertilizer or manure. Most of the phosphorus not taken up by plants remains in the soil and can be used in the future. Phosphorus can be transferred to surface water when it is mined or processed, when excess fertilizer is applied to soil, when soil is eroded, or when effluent is discharged from sewage treatment works. Red arrows show the primary direction of the phosphorus flows; yellow arrows the recycling of phosphorus in the crop and soil system and movement towards water bodies; and grey arrows the phosphorus lost through food wastages in landfills.

(Smil 2000) (**Figure 2**). Farmers also adopted new methods, such as planting high-yielding crop varieties and then applying nutrients—notably nitrogen, phosphorus and potassium (NPK)—and other inputs such as pesticide (Fresco 2009). Scientific progress continued in the last half of the 20th century with the Green Revolution. Although it staved off a great deal of world hunger in the face of significant population growth, the Green Revolution has been criticized for causing environmental damage by encouraging excessive or inappropriate use of fertilizers and other inputs (IFPRI 2002).

To sustain agricultural productivity at current and predicted future levels, it is crucial to determine the full extent of the supply of this finite resource. Thirty-five countries currently produce phosphate rock and it is estimated that 15 others have potentially exploitable resources (IFA 2009). Phosphate rock's value depends on various factors, including physical accessibility,

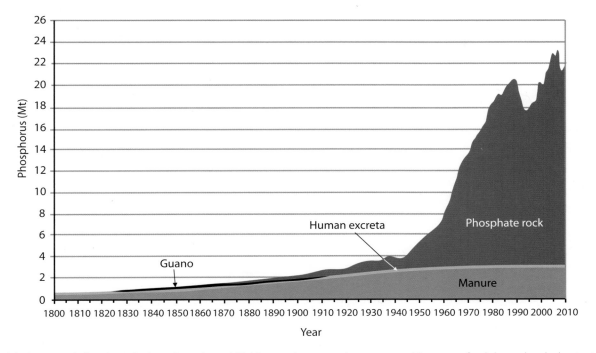

Figure 2: Global sources of phosphorus fertilizer. Since the mid-1940s, population growth accompanied by greater food demand and urbanization have led to a dramatic increase in the use of mined phosphate rock compared with other sources of phosphorus. *Source: Cordell et al. (2009)*

level of impurities and phosphate content. The known supply of cheap, high-grade reserves is becoming increasingly limited while demand continues to increase. The remaining amount of commercially viable phosphate rock, particularly the lifetime of reserves, has been the subject of vigorous debate among experts during the last few years (Vaccari 2009) (**Box 1**).

New phosphate rock mines have been commissioned in several countries, including Australia, Peru and Saudi Arabia, while undiscovered deposits are being widely sought, including in seafloor sediments off the coast of Namibia (Drummond 2010, Jung 2010, Jasinski 2010 and 2011). Although estimates of the extent of known reserves are increasing, the quality of these reserves requires further evaluation. If the phosphate concentration in the rock declines and larger volumes of ore are needed in order to obtain a given amount of phosphorus, production costs will likely increase. Such changes could also lead to greater energy requirements and more waste in phosphate rock mining. In an open market these factors might well raise the price of phosphorus fertilizers, limiting their accessibility to many farmers and having negative effects on yields. If these were to occur, food security could be threatened in countries that are highly dependent on phosphorus imports.

The eradication of hunger and poverty is Goal 1 of the Millennium Declaration, adopted by the United Nations General Assembly in 2000. A 2010 review of progress towards achieving the Millennium Development Goals reported that hunger and malnutrition increased between 2007 and 2009, partially reversing earlier progress (UNGA 2010). Many of the world's estimated 925 million undernourished people are small-scale farmers (IAASTD 2009, FAO 2010). Phosphorus-based fertilizers are often unobtainable by these farmers, whose productivity could be improved with better access to this input (Buresh et al. 1997).

Greater appreciation of the role and value of phosphorus could be the basis for increased co-operation on research and development to acquire a more comprehensive understanding of this essential nutrient—including how it can best be recovered, used and recycled to meet future food demand. Research has already demonstrated the importance of building up and maintaining a critical level of plant-available phosphorus in soil to optimize plant uptake of this nutrient; anything lower than this level would represent a loss of crop yield, and anything higher an unnecessary expense for farmers and a potential cause of phosphorus run-off to receiving waters (Syers et al. 2008). Good

Box 1: The 'peak phosphorus' debate: how long will global phosphate rock reserves last?

The extent of global phosphate rock reserves is difficult to ascertain. Knowledge of phosphate rock deposits is evolving, along with technology and the economics of production (IFDC/UNIDO 1998). How long reserves will last depends on their size, quality and rate of use.

Researchers have raised concern about 'peak phosphorus', the proposition that economic and energy constraints will set a maximum level for phosphate rock production, which will then decrease as demand for phosphorus increases. Many scientists and industry experts contest the specific assertions that have been made regarding when such a peak is likely to occur. For example, Cordell et al. (2009) estimated that peak production of current reserves (that is, phosphate rock known to be economically available for mining and processing) would occur between 2030 and 2040. That estimate was based on United States Geological Survey (USGS) data for global phosphate reserves (Jasinski 2006, 2007 and 2008). Increasingly experts now consider the extent of these reserves to have been underestimated (Van Kauwenbergh 2010). The most recent

USGS estimates have been revised upward (Jasinski 2011). Proponents of the peak phosphorus theory argue that even if the timeline may vary, the fundamental issue, that the supply of cheap and easily accessible phosphorus is ultimately limited, will not change.

A recent report from the International Fertilizer Development Center (IFDC) on reserves and resources provisionally revised the estimate of phosphate rock reserves from the USGS estimate of around 16 billion to approximately 60 billion tonnes (Van Kauwenbergh 2010), which is roughly consistent with the most recent USGS report (Jasinski 2011) (**Figure 3**). These reserves would last 300 to 400 years at current production rates of 160 to 170 million tonnes per year. Since phosphorus fertilizer production is expected to increase by 2 to 3 per cent per year during the next five years, the life expectancy of reserves could be less than that (Heffer and Prud'homme 2010). The IFDC report also estimates that the world's overall phosphate resources amount to approximately 290 billion tonnes and potentially as much as 490 billion tonnes (Van Kauwenbergh 2010).

Phosphate rock is the only new source of phosphorus entering the food production chain. The consistency and volume of food production therefore depend on the accessibility of phosphorus to farmers. Given the difficulties of estimating the longevity of phosphate rock reserves and the vital importance of decision-making based on reliable and transparent information concerning world phosphate rock resources and reserves, IFDC recommends establishing an international, multi-disciplinary network to regularly update a definitive database on phosphate rock deposits (Van Kauwenbergh 2010).

Country	Phosphate rock reserves, millions of tonnes
Morocco	5 700
China	3 700
South Africa	1 500
Jordan	1 500
United States	1 100
Brazil	260
Russia	200
Israel	180
Syria	100
Tunisia	100
Other countries	1 660
World total (rounded)	16 000

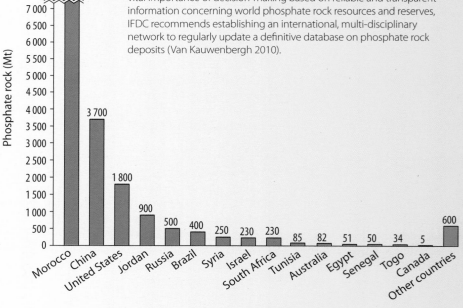

Figure 3: Recent estimates of the distribution of world phosphate rock reserves, as reported by the United States Geological Survey (left) and the International Fertilizer Development Center (right). Most potentially viable phosphate rock reserves are concentrated in a few countries. *Sources: Jasinski (2010) and Van Kauwenbergh (2010)*

Note: The United States Geological Survey's Mineral Commodity Summaries 2011, published on 21 January 2011, revised the USGS estimate of world phosphate rock reserves to 65 billion tonnes. Its revised estimate of Moroccan reserves is 50 billion tonnes, based on information from the Moroccan producer and IFDC. The top ten countries in the 2011 report are Morocco, China (3 700 Mt), Algeria (2 200 Mt), Syria (1 800 Mt), Jordan (1 500 Mt), South Africa (1 500 Mt), the United States (1 400 Mt), Russia (1 300 Mt), Brazil (340 Mt) and Israel (180 Mt). Source: Jasinski (2011)

management practices for fertilizers and agricultural waste products are advocated by many organizations and initiatives, including the International Plant Nutrition Institute and the Global Partnership on Nutrient Management (GPNM 2010).

More sustainable use of a finite resource

Almost 90 per cent of global phosphate rock production is used to produce food and animal feed (Prud'homme 2010). The need for increased agricultural productivity will create higher demand for fertilizer to meet crop requirements by improving supplies of phosphorus, nitrogen and potassium. The specific amounts required will vary with soil type. Phosphorus fertilizer consumption has stabilized in much of the developed world, but it is expected to continue to increase steadily in developing countries (**Figure 4**) (**Box 2**). Population growth will drive much of this demand, but so will increased consumption of meat and dairy products and the cultivation of crops for non-food purposes such as biofuel feedstock (FAO 2008, IFA 2008, Van Vuuren et al. 2010).

Global use of fertilizers that contain phosphorus, nitrogen and potassium increased by 600 per cent between 1950 and 2000 (IFA 2006). This helped to feed a growing world population, but excessive or inappropriate fertilizer use has also led to significant pollution problems in some parts of the world.

In the last half-century, the phosphorus concentrations in freshwater and terrestrial systems have increased by at least 75 per cent while the estimated flow of phosphorus to the ocean from the total land area has risen to 22 million tonnes per year (Bennett et al. 2001). This amount exceeds the world's annual consumption of phosphorus fertilizer, estimated at 18 million tonnes in 2007 (FAOStat 2009). While much of the phosphorus accumulated in terrestrial systems would eventually be available for plant growth, there is no practical way to recover phosphorus lost to aquatic systems.

In aquatic systems too much phosphorus and other nutrients results in eutrophication, which promotes excessive algal and aquatic plant growth along with undesirable impacts on biodiversity, water quality, fish stocks and the recreational

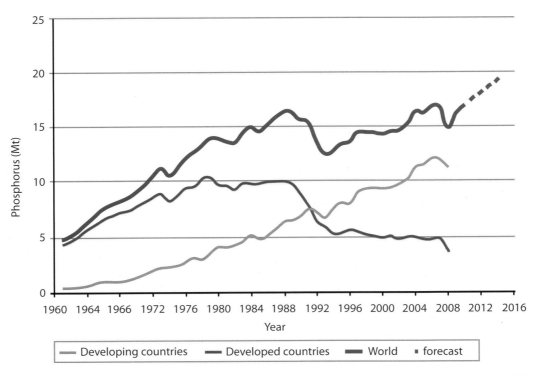

Figure 4: Global phosphorus fertilizer consumption. Demand in developed countries reached a plateau and then declined around 1990. It has continued to increase steadily in developing countries. *Source: Heffer and Prud'homme (2010)*

Box 2: Phosphorus use in African agriculture

Eighty-two per cent of the world's 6.8 billion people live in developing regions (UN 2009). Sixteen per cent of the population in these regions is chronically undernourished (UN 2010), which in some regions can largely be linked to soils' low productive capacity. For example, in Africa nearly three-quarters of farmland is depleted of nutrients, lowering crop yield to one-quarter of the global average (Henao and Baanante 2006). At the same time, more nutrients continue to be removed each year than are added in the form of fertilizer, crop residues and manure.

Nutrient balance studies in the 1990s suggested average annual depletion rates of 22 kg nitrogen (N), 2.5 kg phosphorus (P) and 15 kg potassium (K) per hectare in Africa. Intensively cultivated highlands in East Africa lose an estimated 36 kg N, 5 kg P and 25 kg K per hectare per year, while croplands in the Sahel lose 10 kg N, 2 kg P and 8 kg K per hectare (Smaling et al. 1997). Average annual fertilizer use in Africa is only about 17 kg per hectare, compared, for example, to 96 kg per hectare in Latin America (**Figure 5**). Even this low rate of consumption is restricted to just a few African countries. Sub-Saharan Africa, excluding South Africa, uses about 5 kilograms of fertilizer per hectare per year, of which less than 30 per cent is phosphorus. These levels are insufficient to balance offtake in crop products.

A combination of high cost and low accessibility prevents many African farmers from acquiring fertilizer. Poor transport, low trade volumes, and lack of local production or distribution capacity result in farm-gate fertilizer prices two to six times higher than the world average. Nevertheless, fertilizer is needed to achieve adequate sustainable crop yields. The Africa Fertilizer Summit (2006) concluded that a lasting solution requires policies to sustain robust distribution networks, including adequate credit sources, retail outlets and transportation, as well as the transfer of technology and knowledge for efficient fertilizer use.

A more sustainable strategy would include integrated soil nutrient management to make the most of organic sources of phosphorus, such as crop residues, animal manure and food waste, combined with more judicious use of mineral phosphorus fertilizers (Alley and Vanlauwe 2009). This would result in multiple environmental benefits, including erosion control. Run-off and erosion combined are responsible for 48 and 40 per cent of phosphorus losses in intensively cultivated highland areas and in parts of the Sahel, respectively (Smaling et al. 1997).

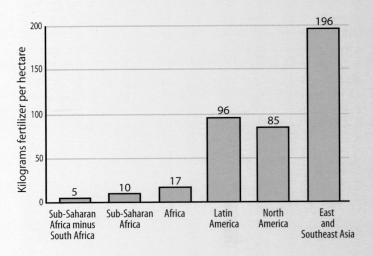

Figure 5: Regional disparities in the application of fertilizers containing nitrogen, phosphorus and potassium. *Source: IFA (2009)*

---

value of the environment. Algal blooms can include species that release toxins which are harmful to humans or animals, while decomposition of algae can lower dissolved oxygen levels, causing mass mortality among fish (Carpenter et al. 1998, MA 2005). Scientists have warned that human-induced nutrient over-enrichment can push aquatic ecosystems beyond natural thresholds, causing abrupt shifts in ecosystem structure and functioning (Rockström et al. 2009).

The estimated annual cost of eutrophication in the United States alone is as high as US$2.2 billion (Dodds et al. 2009). This problem is exacerbated in countries' large urban centres, where phosphorus from excreta and detergents is concentrated in wastewater streams and discharged along with nitrogen and other nutrients. If local authorities do not invest in facilities to remove these nutrients, they will be discharged with other effluent into rivers and other water bodies (Van Drecht et al. 2009). This

is frequently the case in the mega-cities in developing countries, where more than 70 per cent of wastewater enters surface or groundwater untreated (Nyenje et al. 2010).

In many parts of the world, traditional nutrient cycles that were once the basis of local food production, consumption and waste management have changed in response to the need to produce more food in a globalizing world. Over four times as much phosphorus flows through the environment than before phosphorus fertilizer began to be used in agriculture (Smil 2002). Soils that receive phosphorus retain a high proportion, but the variability of the world's soils makes this amount difficult to assess, particularly at large scales. Agricultural efficiency—especially in the expanding area of livestock management—will be essential to optimize phosphorus use, avoid nutrient losses and meet increasingly strict environmental regulations. For example, the European Union's Water Framework Directive requires potential pollutants to be removed from wastewater prior to disposal into surface water. Sustainable land management is important for the prevention of phosphorus loss to water bodies resulting from soil erosion. Improved technologies to remove impurities such as heavy metals from fertilizer products would also minimize their transfer to agricultural soils or surface waters.

Using phosphate rock more sustainably would help ensure its long-term economic viability and the availability of phosphorus to farmers. Because phosphorus flows through the global food system, there are options for enhancing efficiency at each stage of the value chain. They include lengthening the life of reserves through improvements in mining (**Box 3**), in fertilizer production and in fertilizer use efficiency. Recycling phosphorus from excreta or other organic wastes also presents an important opportunity

to recover this nutrient. Given the diversity of phosphorus-related issues, an environmentally integrated set of policy options and technical measures is required to ensure more sustainable use of this essential resource.

Soil erosion is a natural process significantly accelerated by human activity, particularly land use changes such as deforestation. Overgrazing or removal of vegetation leaves the soil unprotected and vulnerable to the effects of rain. Soils are particularly prone to erosion in tropical and subtropical regions, where rainfall is usually higher and more intense. Rates of erosion vary with the type of soil and landscape.

A number of measures can be taken to enhance the efficiency of phosphorus use and reduce phosphorus losses, such as effective land management to help reduce losses due to soil erosion (**Box 4**).

Eutrophication of Lake Winnipeg in Manitoba, Canada. Ongoing efforts to improve the lake's health include reducing nutrient inflow from wastewater, eliminating fertilizer use in buffer zones, and reducing phosphorus content in household detergents. *Credit: Lori Volkart*

Box 3: Improving the sustainability of phosphorus mining

The environmental performance of the fertilizer raw material industry has improved in recent decades, with a greater focus on sustainability in the mining sector. New management systems have been responsible for improved environmental performance, which also yields economic benefits. Increasing phosphorus recovery during mining operations can extend the life expectancy of reserves (Prud'homme 2010).

The area affected by surface mining operations varies with ore-body geometry and thickness. The phosphate content of the ore is upgraded by concentration, or 'beneficiation'. This process removes contaminants such as clay and other fine particles, organic matter, and siliceous and iron-bearing minerals (UNEP/IFA 2001). Such materials are usually removed by crushing/grinding, scrubbing, water washing and screening. They end up in water bodies, mined-out areas or specially designed ponds.

As with many mining activities, the extraction and beneficiation of phosphate rock has potential negative environmental impacts, including damage to the landscape, excessive water consumption, water contamination and air pollution. These impacts are localized and are mostly limited to the mining site (UNEP/IFA 2001). A range of landscaping practices are used to minimize disturbance and accelerate the re-establishment of vegetation, while wastes are confined to a specific area, providing a high degree of management control.

Work is currently under way to recycle process water, reclaim fines, and treat the waste stream to increase the recovery rate. However, information on phosphorus recovery in mining and ore beneficiation is lacking. Reported rates vary widely, with values ranging between 41 and 95 per cent (Prud'homme 2010, Van Kauwenbergh 2010).

Open-cast mining of phosphate rock in Togo. Most of the world's phosphate rock is extracted from open pits, as shown here, or from large-scale mines equipped with drag lines or shovel/excavator systems. *Credit: Alexandra Pugachevsky*

Box 4: Managing soil erosion to minimize phosphorus losses

Since plant nutrients are concentrated in the topsoil, removal of surface soil through erosion can greatly reduce soil productivity. Siltation and eutrophication also damage the aquatic environment. Thus, protecting topsoil from soil erosion maintains soil productivity and conserves water quality.

Measured rates of erosion and sediment transport vary. Topsoil removal rates of 0.47 tonnes per hectare per year have been measured in Africa, compared with rates almost four times as high in Asia (El Swaify et al. 1982). Due to the cost of making measurements, erosion simulation models have been developed. However, these models often provide different results when applied at different spatial scales.

Some 75 to 90 per cent of the phosphorus lost in surface run-off from cropped land is associated with soil particles (Sharpley and Rekolainen 1997). In Africa total annual phosphorus removal by all pathways is estimated at 2.5 kilograms per hectare, while phosphorus loss due to erosion and run-off is approximately 1 kilogram per hectare per year (Smaling et al. 1997).

Several well-recognized practices can minimize soil erosion, such as contour ploughing carried out parallel to the land's contours rather than up or down slopes, and contour planting of hedgerows on steep land. Since it is vegetation cover that principally determines the extent of soil loss by erosion, the long-term solution to control erosion rates is through vegetation protection, including use of mulches, cover crops, and fertility-enhancing systems on low-fertility soil (Stocking 1984). These practices have the potential to be more widely adopted in the developing world, although they are limited by lack of land tenure, the costs of adopting them, limited extension support and other socio-economic factors. Improved farmer education is an important starting point.

Major gains can be made through improving plant nutrient management and recycling phosphorus from waste streams (Syers et al. 2008, Gilbert 2009, Van Vuuren et al. 2010). Technological innovations in waste management can dramatically lower the amount of phosphorus making its way into the aquatic environment (**Box 5**). Such improvements sometimes produce co-benefits such as energy generation from biogas (Van Vuuren et al. 2010). Recycling sewage sludge is another option, although there are some health concerns as sludge may contain high concentrations of heavy metals, pathogens and other contaminants.

Some European countries are already formulating targets for phosphorus recycling. For example, Sweden aims to recycle 60 per cent of the phosphorus in municipal wastewater by 2015 (Swedish Environmental Protection Agency 2010).

Box 5: From waste to phosphorus recovery and recycling

For centuries, animal and human excreta have been added to farmland to supply nutrients for growing crops. Farmers in most parts of the world still consider animal manure a valuable soil amendment. To recover nutrients, including the phosphorus in human excreta, a wide range of technologies are being developed, ranging from low-cost, small-scale systems to expensive high-technology ones.

'Ecological sanitation' recovery systems for human excreta are designed to close nutrient and water cycles. For example, nutrient recycling from human waste can be achieved using urine-diverting dry toilets (Morgan 2007). Such on-site systems are particularly appropriate in rural and peri-urban areas, where households are not connected to sewerage or farmers do not have access to—or cannot afford—chemical fertilizers (Rosemarin et al. 2008). Trials in villages in Niger by Dagerskog and Bonzi (2010) found that an average rural family of nine persons excreted the equivalent of chemical fertilizer worth about US$80 per year. The urine component produced comparable or 10 to 20 per cent higher yields of sorghum and millet, compared to the same amount of nutrients applied as chemical fertilizer.

Interest in recycling phosphorus and other nutrients from sanitation systems has been increasing for several years (Esrey et al. 2001). Responding to this interest, the World Health Organization has developed guidelines for the safe reuse of human excreta in agriculture (WHO 2006).

Other innovations in the area of ecological sanitation have significantly increased the feasibility of extracting phosphorus from municipal wastewater streams (Gantenbein and Khadka 2009, Tilley et al. 2009). The output is the mineral struvite, a white solid formed when bacteria are used to clean up sludge. Struvite has demonstrated value as a source of phosphorus-based fertilizer (Johnston and Richards 2003). First used commercially in 2007, this technology is currently in full-scale use in treatment plants in some major cities in North America and the United Kingdom.

During the past decade, researchers have started to focus on reducing phosphorus losses by developing ways to improve phosphorus uptake by animals. In particular, intensive pig rearing produces massive volumes of phosphorus-rich manure. Monogastric animals such as the pig are unable to break down phytate, the major form of phosphorus in their feed. Phosphorus is therefore added to their diet as an inorganic supplement, but much of it is excreted due to low uptake in the gut. Scientists at the University of Guelph in Canada have developed a genetically engineered *Enviropig* able to digest phytate (Forsberg et al. 2003). This decreases the need for an inorganic phosphorus supplement. Other research groups are developing low-phytate crops or focusing on the production of phytase, an enzyme that helps animals to digest phytate.

Technological innovation has resulted in the development of a pig able to digest phytate. This reduces the need to provide a phosphorus supplement, much of which is excreted. Approval by the Canadian government in early 2010 allowed farmers to begin raising the *Enviropig*, a significant step towards enabling its processing and sale as food. *Credit: University of Guelph*

Scrubbing and washing with seawater of phosphate rock in the coastal area of Togo. *Credit: Takehiro Nakamura*

Population growth and economic development are expected to further increase agricultural production, particularly livestock raising. Future demand for phosphorus will strongly depend on the types of agricultural practices that accompany this increase (Vitousek et al. 2009). Dietary changes and reduction of food waste in the retail sector and households would help reduce phosphorus losses, and would require greater awareness and a change in attitude in order to alter consumption patterns. As promising options emerge, they will call for decision making based on reliable scientific evidence derived from further research on phosphorus availability, product flows and end-uses (Hilton et al. 2010, Van Vuuren et al. 2010).

Looking ahead

Phosphorus has received only limited attention compared to other important agricultural inputs such as nitrogen and water. Because of the vital role of phosphorus in food production, any consideration of food security needs to include an informed discussion concerning more sustainable use of this limited resource. Key themes include the increasing global demand for phosphorus fertilizers, the ongoing debate over the long-term availability of phosphate rock, lack of adequate phosphorus accessibility by many of the world's farmers, prospects for increased recycling and more efficient phosphorus use in agriculture, and minimization of losses through soil erosion

control. More detailed research is required to provide reliable, global-scale quantification of the amount of phosphorus available for food production. A global phosphorus assessment, including further insights from scientists and other experts, policy-makers and other stakeholders, could contribute to improving fertilizer accessibility, waste management in urban settings, and recycling of phosphorus from food waste and from animal and human excreta.

The long-term availability of phosphorus for global food production is of fundamental importance to the world population. Given the diversity of issues surrounding phosphorus, only an integrated set of policy options and technical measures can ensure its efficient and sustainable use. Environmental solutions that improve nutrient management and recycling, minimize phosphorus losses due to soil erosion, and foster sustainable production and consumption also promote wise use of a finite resource. This could be the basis for fostering environmental innovation and other actions at local, national, regional and international levels to improve phosphorus management. The future of this resource will also depend on governance with regard to its extraction and distribution around the world. There is a need for accurate information about the extent of global reserves, new technologies, infrastructure, institutions, attitudes and policies to meet the challenge of sustainably feeding a rapidly growing global population while maintaining a healthy and productive environment.

References

Africa Fertilizer Summit (2006). *Africa Fertilizer Summit Proceedings*. International Fertilizer Development Center (IFDC), Muscle Shoals, Alabama, USA

Alley, M.M. and Vanlauwe, B. (2009). *The Role of Fertilizers in Integrated Plant Nutrient Management*. International Fertilizer Industry Association (IFA), Paris, and Tropical Soil Biology and Fertility Institute of the International Centre for Tropical Agriculture (TSBF-CIAT), Nairobi

Bennett, E.M., Carpenter, S.R. and Caraco, N.F. (2001). Human impact on erodable phosphorus and eutrophication: A global perspective. *Bioscience*, 51(3), 227-234

Buresh, R.J., Smithson, P.C. and Heliums, D.T. (1997). Building Soil Phosphorus Capital in Africa. In: Buresh, R.J., Sanchez, P.A. and Calhoun, F. (eds.), *Replenishing Soil Fertility in Africa*. Special Publication No. 51. Soil Science Society of America (SSSA) and American Society of Agronomy (ASA), Madison, Wisconsin, USA

Carpenter, S.R., Caraco, N.F., Correll, D.L., Howarth, R.W., Sharpley, A.N. and Smith, V.H. (1998). Nonpoint pollution of surface waters with phosphorus and nitrogen. *Ecological Applications*, 8(3), 559-568

Cordell, D., Drangert, J.-O. and White, S. (2009). The Story of Phosphorus: Global food security and food for thought. *Global Environmental Change*, 19, 292-305

Dagerskog, L. and Bonzi, M. (2010). Opening minds and closing loops – productive sanitation initiatives in Burkina Faso and Niger. *Sustainable Sanitation Practice*, 3

Dodds, W.K., Bouska, W.W., Eitzmann, J.L., Pilger, T.J., Pitts, K.L., Riley, A.J. and Thornbrugh, D.J. (2009). Eutrophication of US Freshwaters: Analysis of Potential Economic Damages. *Environmental Science & Technology*, 43(1), 12-19

Drecht, G. van, Bouwman, A.F., Harrison, J. and Knoop, J.M. (2009). Global nitrogen and phosphate in urban wastewater for the period 1970 to 2050. *Global Biogeochemical Cycles*, 23

Drummond, A. (2010). Minemakers: Targeting Phosphate Production from Two Continents. Paper presented at the Phosphates 2010 International Conference, 22-24 March, Brussels

El-Swaify, S.A., Dangler, E.W. and Armstrong, C.L. (1982). *Soil erosion by water in the tropics*. Research Extension Series 024, College of Tropical Agriculture and Human Resources, University of Hawaii

Esrey, S., Andersson, I., Hillers, A. and Sawyer, R. (2001). *Closing the Loop: Ecological sanitation for food security*. Publication on Water Resources No. 18. United Nations Development Programme (UNDP) and Swedish International Development Cooperation Agency (SIDA)

FAO (2008). Soaring food prices: facts, perspectives, impacts and actions required. Presented at the High-level Conference on World Food Security: The Challenges of Climate Change and Bioenergy, 3-5 June 2008, Food and Agriculture Organization of the United Nations, Rome

FAO (2010). *The State of Food Insecurity in the World 2010: Addressing food insecurity in protracted crises*. Food and Agriculture Organization of the United Nations, Rome

FAOStat (2009). Online database providing time-series and cross sectional data relating to food and agriculture for some 200 countries. Food and Agriculture Organization of the United Nations, Rome. http://faostat.fao.org

Forsberg, C.W., Phillips, J.P., Golovan, S.P., Fan, M.Z., Meidinger, R.G., Ajakaiye, A., Hilborn, D. and Hacker, R.R. (2003). The Enviropig physiology, performance, and contribution to nutrient management advances in a regulated environment: The leading edge of change in the pork industry. *Journal of Animal Science*, 81, 68-77

Fresco, L. (2009). Challenges for food system adaptation today and tomorrow. *Environmental Science & Policy*, 12, 2009, 378-385

Gantenbein, B. and Khadka, R. (2009). *Struvite Recovery from Urine at Community Scale in Nepal. Final Project Report Phase I*. Swiss Federal Institute of Aquatic Science and Technology (Eawag), Duebendorf, Switzerland, and UN-Habitat Water for Asian Cities Programme Nepal, Kathmandu

Gilbert, N. (2009). The disappearing nutrient. *Nature*, 461, 716-718

GPNM (2010). *Building the foundations for sustainable nutrient management. A publication of the Global Partnership on Nutrient Management*. Published by the United Nations Environment Programme on behalf of the Global Partnership on Nutrient Management

Heffer, P. and Prud'homme, M. (2010). *Fertilizer Outlook 2010-2014*, 78th IFA Annual Conference, 31 May-2 June 2010, International Fertilizer Industry Association (IFA), Paris

Henao, J. and Baanante, C. (2006). *Agricultural Production and Soil Nutrient Mining in Africa: Implications for Resource Conservation and Policy Development*. International Fertilizer Development Center (IFDC), Muscle Shoals, Alabama, USA

Hilton, J., Johnston, A.E. and Dawson, C.J. (2010). *The Phosphate Life-Cycle: Rethinking the Options for a Finite Resource*. Proceedings No. 668. International Fertiliser Society, Leek, UK

IAASTD (2009). *Agriculture at a Crossroads: Synthesis Report*. International Assessment of Knowledge, Science and Technology for Development

IFA (2006). *Production and International Trade Statistics*. International Fertilizer Industry Association, Paris

IFA (2008). *Feeding the Earth: Fertilizers and Global Food Security, Market Drivers and Fertilizer Economics*. International Fertilizer Industry Association, Paris

IFA (2009). Annual Phosphate Rock Statistics. International Fertilizer Industry Association, Paris

IFDC/UNIDO (1998). *Fertilizer Manual*. Prepared by the International Fertilizer Development Center (IFDC) and the United Nations Industrial Development Organization (UNIDO). Kluwer Academic Publishers, Dordrecht, the Netherlands

IFPRI (2002). *GREEN REVOLUTION: Curse or Blessing?* International Food Policy Research Institute, Washington, D.C.

Jacob, K.D. (1964). Predecessors of superphosphate. In: United States Department of Agriculture and Tennessee Valley Authority (TVA), *Superphosphate: its history, chemistry and manufacture*. United States Government Printing Office, Washington, D.C.

Jasinski, S.M. (2006). Phosphate Rock. In: *Mineral Commodity Summaries 2006*. United States Geological Survey. United States Government Printing Office, Washington, D.C.

Jasinski, S.M. (2007). Phosphate Rock. In: *Mineral Commodity Summaries 2007*. United States Geological Survey. United States Government Printing Office, Washington, D.C.

Jasinski, S.M. (2008). Phosphate Rock. In: *Mineral Commodity Summaries 2008*. United States Geological Survey. United States Government Printing Office, Washington, D.C.

Jasinski, S.M. (2010). Phosphate Rock. In: *Mineral Commodity Summaries 2010*. United States Geological Survey. United States Government Printing Office, Washington, D.C.

Jasinski, S.M. (2011). Phosphate Rock. In: *Mineral Commodity Summaries 2011*. United States Geological Survey. United States Government Printing Office, Washington, D.C.

Johnston, A.E. and Richards, I.R. (2003). Effectiveness of different precipitated phosphates as phosphorus sources for plants. *Soil Use and Management*, 19, 45-49

Jung, A. (2010). Phosphates Fertilizer Outlook, British Sulphur Consultants. Paper presented at the Phosphates 2010 International Conference, 22-24 March, 2010, Brussels

Kauwenbergh, S. Van. (2010). *World Phosphate Rock Reserves and Resources, IFDC Technical Bulletin 75*. International Fertilizer Development Center (IFDC), Muscle Shoals, Alabama, USA

MA (2005). Nutrient Cycling. Chapter 12 in: Hassan, R., Scholes, R. and Ash, N. (eds.), *Ecosystems and Human Well-Being: Current State and Trends, Volume 1. Millennium Ecosystem Assessment*. Island Press, Washington, D.C.

Morgan, P. (2007). Toilets That Make Compost: Low-cost, sanitary toilets that produce valuable compost for crops in an African context. Stockholm Environment Institute

Nyenje, P.M., Foppen, J.W., Uhlenbrook, S., Kulabako, R. and Muwanga, A. (2010). Eutrophication and nutrient release in urban areas of sub-Saharan Africa – A review. *Science of the Total Environment*, 408(3), 447-455

Prud'homme, M. (2010). *World Phosphate Rock Flows, Losses and Uses*. Paper presented at the Phosphates 2010 Conference and Exhibition, Brussels, March 2010

Rockström, J., Steffen, W., Noone, K., Persson, A., Chapin, F.S., Lambin, E.F. and Foley, J.A. (2009). A safe operating space for humanity. *Nature*, 461(7263), 472-475

Rosemarin, A., Ekane, N., Caldwell, I., Kvarnström, E., McConville, J., Ruben, C. and Fogde, M. (2008). *Pathways for Sustainable Sanitation: Achieving the Millennium Development Goals*. Stockholm Environment Institute. IWA Publishing, London

Schröder, J.J., Cordell, D., Smit, A.L. and Rosemarin, R. (2010). *Sustainable Use of Phosphorous*. Report No. 357. Plant Research International, Wageningen University and Research Centre, the Netherlands, and Stockholm Environment Institute

Sharpley, A. and Rekolainen, S. (1997). Phosphorus in Agriculture and Its Environmental Implications. In: Tunney, H., Carton, O.T., Brookes, P.C. and Johnston, A.E. (eds.), *Phosphorus Loss from Soil to Water*. CAB International, Wallingford, UK

Smaling, E.M.A., Nandwa, S.M. and Janssen, B.H. (1997). Soil fertility in Africa is at stake. In: Buresh, R.J., Sanchez, P.A. and Calhoun, F. (eds.), *Replenishing Soil Fertility in Africa*. Special Publication No. 51. Soil Science Society of America (SSSA) and American Society of Agronomy, Madison, Wisconsin, USA

Smil, V. (2000). Phosphorus in the Environment: Natural Flows and Human Interferences. *Annual Review of Energy and the Environment*, 25, 53-88

Smil, V. (2002). Phosphorus: Global Transfers. In: Douglas, I. (ed.), *Encyclopedia of Global Environmental Change, Volume 3, Causes and Consequences of Global Environmental Change*. John Wiley & Sons, Chichester, UK

Stocking, M. (1984). Rates of erosion and sediment yield in the African environment. In: Walling, D.E., Foster, S.S.D. and Wurzel, P. (eds.), *Challenges in African Hydrology and Water Resources* (Proceedings of the Harare Workshop Symposium in July 1984). International Association of Hydrological Sciences (IAHS) Publication No. 14

Swedish Environmental Protection Agency (2010). *Reporting of government assignment 21: Update of the "Action Plan for Reuse of Phosphorus from Wastewater"*. Ministry of Environment, Stockholm

Syers, J.K., Johnston, A.E. and Curtin, D.C. (2008). *Efficiency of Soil and Fertilizer Phosphorus Use*. FAO Fertilizer and Plant Nutrition Bulletin 18

Tilley. E., Gantenbein, B., Khadka, R., Zurbrügg, C. and Udert, K.M. (2009). Social and Economic Feasibility of Struvite Recovery from Urine at the Community Level in Nepal. In: Ashley, K., Mavinic, D. and Koch, F. (eds.), *International Conference on Nutrient Recovery from Wastewater Streams*. IWA Publishing, London

UN (2009). *World Population Prospects: The 2008 Revision*. Highlights. Population Division of the Department of Economic and Social Affairs of the United Nations Secretariat, United Nations, New York

UN (2010). *The Millennium Development Goals Report*. United Nations Department of Economic and Social Affairs, United Nations, New York2008

UNEP/IFA (2001). *Environmental Aspects of Phosphate and Potash Mining*. United Nations Environment Programme and International Fertilizer Industry Association (IFA), Paris

UNGA (2010). *Keeping the promise: United to achieve the MDGs. A forward-looking review to promote an agreed action agenda to achieve the Millennium Development Goals by 2015*. United Nations General Assembly 64/665

Vaccari, D.A. (2009). Phosphorus Famine: The Threat to Our Food Supply. *Scientific American*, June, 54-59

Vitousek, P.M., Naylor, R., Crews, T., David, M.B., Drinkwater, L.E., Holland, E., Johnes, P.J., Katzenberger, J., Martinelli, L.A., Matson, P.A., Nziguheba, G., Ojima, D., Palm, C.A., Robertson, G.P., Sanchez, P.A., Townsend, A.R. and Zhang, F.S. (2009). Nutrient imbalances in agricultural development. *Science* 324(5934), 1519-1520

Vuuren, D.P.Van, Bouwman, A.F. and Beusen, A.H.W. (2010) Phosphorus demand for the 1970-2100 period: A scenario analysis of resource depletion. *Global Environmental Change*, 20, 428-439

WHO (2006). *Guidelines for the safe use of wastewater, excreta and greywater. Volume 4: Excreta and greywater use in agriculture*. World Health Organization, Geneva

There is a new level of awareness of the global importance of forests and sustainable forest management. *Credit: Rowland Williams*

Emerging Perspectives on Forest Biodiversity

Forests are the focus of renewed global attention because of their role in climate change mitigation. However, biodiversity loss continues to put forests at risk, diminishing their capacity to adapt to pressures, including climate change. New approaches to biodiversity conservation are promising, but they need to be matched by more effective governance and greater financial investments.

The world's forests play an important role in maintaining fundamental ecological processes, such as water regulation and carbon storage, as well as in providing livelihoods and supporting economic growth (UNEP 2007, FAO 2009a). About 1.6 billion people depend in some way on forests for their livelihoods, and wood and other goods removed from forests were valued at US$122 billion in 2005 (World Bank 2004, FAO 2010). As the home of two-thirds of all plants and animals living on land, forests are the most biodiverse terrestrial ecosystems (Schmitt et al. 2009, FAO 2010, IUCN 2010). Many of the essential benefits we derive from forests are underpinned by forest biodiversity, as is the capacity of forests to adapt to pressures, including climate change (MA 2005a, Seppala et al. 2009).

There is a new level of awareness of the global importance of forests and sustainable forest management. Reducing greenhouse gas emissions from deforestation—and reducing forest degradation—are recognized as central to achieving the

What is forest biodiversity?

Forests are defined as land with tree crown cover (or equivalent stocking level) of more than 10 per cent and an area of more than 0.5 hectares (FAO 2000).

Forest biodiversity is the variability among living organisms in forest ecosystems. It comprises diversity within and among species, and within and between each of the terrestrial and aquatic components of forest ecosystems (CBD 1992).

objectives of the UN Framework Convention on Climate Change (UNFCCC) (**Box 1**). Investing in sustainable forest management can also create millions of new 'green jobs' (FAO 2009b). For more than 20 years, the international community has demonstrated its concern about deforestation, forest degradation, and the consequent loss of forest biodiversity (FAO 2009a, Rayner et al. 2010). Progress at the international level has included adoption of the Convention on Biological Diversity, and has been complemented by efforts at the national and sub-national levels. Thirteen per cent of the world's total forest area is under formal protection, and almost 75 per cent of forests are covered by a national forest programme. There is also an upsurge in sustainable forest management initiatives and the strengthening of local rights with regard to forest management at the local level (FAO 2007, Agrawal et al. 2008, CBD 2010, FAO 2010).

Despite this progress, and net gains in forest area in Europe and Asia, total loss of forest cover during the last decade still averaged around 13 million hectares per year (FAO 2010) (**Figure 1**). Most deforestation is occurring in tropical forests, which are especially

Box 1: Forest biodiversity and climate change mitigation

Trees sequester and store carbon from the atmosphere. Although the link between biodiversity and carbon cycling is not well understood, one-quarter of the carbon emitted by human activities, such as burning of fossil fuels, is thought to be fixed by forests and other land ecosystems (Midgley et al. 2010). Forests therefore play an important role in addressing climate change. **REDD+** is an international policy mechanism whose purpose is to mitigate climate change by **R**educing **E**missions from **D**eforestation and forest **D**egradation in developing countries, and to enhance forest carbon stocks through activities such as forest conservation and sustainable forest management (Angelsen 2009). Paying developing countries to conserve forests highlights the economic importance of ecosystems and biodiversity. With the UN Development Programme and the UN's Food and Agricultural Organization, UNEP is assisting countries to participate in REDD+.

Authors: Richard Fleming (co-chair), Peter Kanowski (co-chair), Nick Brown, Jan Jenik, Paula Kahumbu and Jan Plesnik
Science writer: Tahia Devisscher

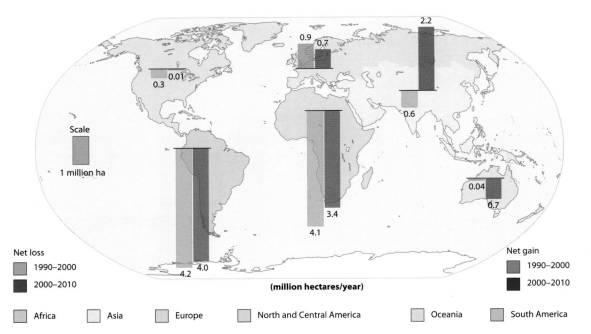

Figure 1: Annual change in forest area by region in millions of hectares per year, 1990-2010. There is a continued trend towards expansion in Europe, while large-scale afforestation in China of between 2 and 3 million hectares per year is contributing to net gains in Asia. The rate of deforestation is decreasing in some countries, such as Brazil and Indonesia. However, net losses remain significant in South America and Africa despite this reduction. Severe drought and forest fires have exacerbated forest losses in Australia since 2000. *Source: FAO (2010)*

rich in biodiversity (CBD 2010). Although the global rate of net forest cover loss has slowed, partly due to the expansion of plantations and to natural forest restoration, forest biodiversity loss continues to occur disproportionately since the highest levels of deforestation and of forest degradation are reported for biodiversity-rich natural forests in developing countries (Schulze et al. 2004, CBD 2010).

The greater scientific, management and political focus on forest biodiversity conservation is offering new understanding, insights and opportunities for responding more effectively to forest biodiversity loss (MA 2005a, Cashore et al. 2006, Gardner et al. 2010, Maris and Béchet 2010, Pfund 2010).

Drivers and consequences of forest biodiversity loss

Globally, the key drivers of forest biodiversity loss are: population and consumption growth; increasing trade in food and agricultural products; growing demand for forest products, including biomass for energy generation; expansion of human settlements and infrastructure; and climate change (FAO 2009, Slingenberg et al. 2009, DeFries et al. 2010, IUCN 2010). At the landscape scale, these drivers are manifested in biodiversity loss resulting from pressures such as deforestation for agriculture and development, fragmentation of forest habitats, forest degradation associated with unsustainable harvesting of forest products for industrial use and livelihood needs, changed fire regimes, an increase in invasive

species, and proliferation of pests and diseases (Asner et al. 2005, FAO 2007, UNEP 2007, Nellemann and Corcoran 2010).

If current global trends in habitat loss, resource exploitation and climate change continue, rates of species extinction will accelerate, biodiversity-rich habitats will be lost or degraded, especially in the tropics, and the distribution and abundance of species and ecosystems will change dramatically (Lindenmayer et al. 2008, Leadley et al. 2010). **Figure 2** shows the outcome of a scenario for human impacts on biodiversity to 2050 (Alkemade et al. 2009).

Loss of forest biodiversity diminishes forest ecosystems' resilience, that is, their ability to adapt to and recover from natural and human-induced disturbance. This can adversely affect both local livelihoods and national economies (MA 2005b). Societal changes, such as those associated with increasing wealth and consumption, may further intensify pressures on forests (Haines-Young and Potschin 2009). Many pressures are expected to be amplified by climate change (Malhi et al. 2009). For example, there is growing concern that changes in climate could occur so rapidly that many forest species will not be able to adapt and migrate (Menéndez et al. 2006). The capacity of individual species to migrate and colonize new environments depends on the characteristics of both species and landscapes. Landscape fragmentation, which results in less connectivity of habitat to allow natural migration, limits the adaptive capacity of species and the viability of ecosystems (Vos et al. 2008).

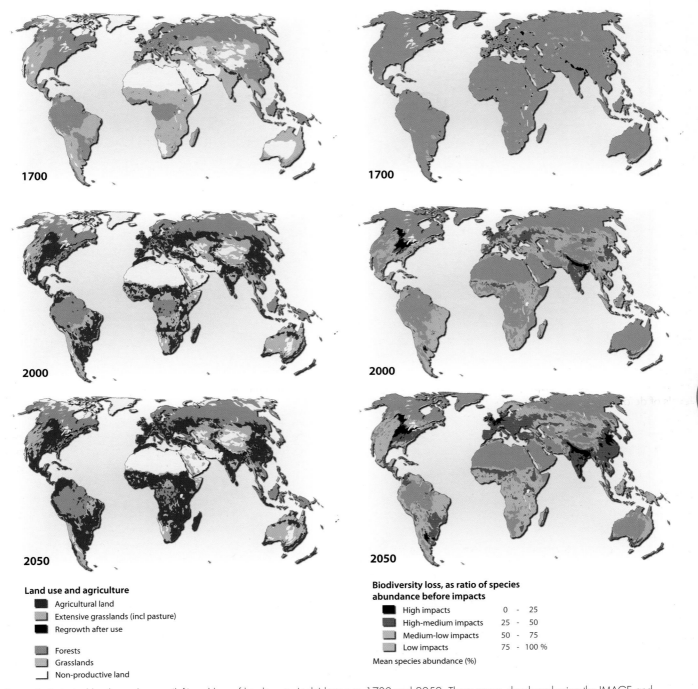

1700

1700

2000

2000

2050

2050

Land use and agriculture

- Agricultural land
- Extensive grasslands (incl pasture)
- Regrowth after use

- Forests
- Grasslands
- Non-productive land

Biodiversity loss, as ratio of species abundance before impacts

High impacts	0 - 25
High-medium impacts	25 - 50
Medium-low impacts	50 - 75
Low impacts	75 - 100 %

Mean species abundance (%)

Figure 2: Projected land use changes (left) and loss of biodiversity (right) between 1700 and 2050. These maps, developed using the IMAGE and GLOBIO3 models, show increasing impacts on forest biodiversity driven by land-use intensity, land cover change, fragmentation, infrastructure development, atmospheric nitrogen deposition and climate change. *Sources: IMAGE, GLOBIO3 and Alkemade et al. (2009), reproduced in Nellemann et al. (2010) Credit: Hugo Ahlenius, Nordpil*

Aerial view showing extensive tree mortality of mature lodgepole pine in British Columbia, Canada, as a result of mountain pine beetle attack. Credit: L. Maclauchlan, British Columbia Ministry of Forests and Range. Credit moutain pine beetle: Dion Manastyrski

Box 2: Pest outbreaks in boreal forests

The mountain pine beetle (*Dendroctonus ponderosae*) is endemic to North American pine forests, where it persists in small populations that can only survive in wounded or otherwise weakened host pines. When there are enough beetles to overcome the resistance of healthy, mature pines during a mass-attack, a population eruption of the insect becomes possible. If subsequent generations of beetles successfully mass-attack additional mature pines, the population eruption can spread through the stand. The potential for such eruptions increases with the beetles' winter survival and the proportion of suitable host trees within the stand. A regional outbreak can develop if the eruption then spreads from its stand of origin outwards to the broader landscape. This becomes more likely with increasing connectedness and prevalence of suitable host stands in the landscape.

Since 2000, the mountain pine beetle outbreak in North America has killed over 14 million hectares of mature pines in Canada and 4 million hectares in the United States (Alfaro et al. 2010). Among the factors contributing to the outbreak are decades of forest management, including fire suppression and planting, that favoured mature lodgepole pine. The area occupied by these pines had more than tripled at the start of the outbreak (Taylor and Carroll 2004). The unprecedented extensiveness of mature pine—the preferred host tree—combined with unusually high beetle survival during a series of mild winters allowed the current outbreak to become much more severe and extensive than any previously recorded (Carroll et al. 2004, Safranyik and Carroll 2006, Taylor et al. 2006) (**Figure 3**). The mountain pine beetle was unable to spread across the landscape to the same extent during earlier outbreaks because the connectedness and contiguity of suitable host stands were broken up by younger pines and greater diversity of tree species (Taylor et al. 2006, Raffa et al. 2008).

The mountain pine beetle outbreak was a factor contributing to the collapse of timber industries, leaving many forestry industry-based towns in British Columbia with depressed economies, failed small businesses, high unemployment and dwindling populations as people started to look for jobs elsewhere.

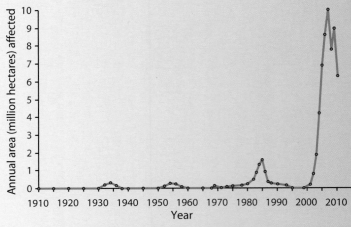

Figure 3: Millions of hectares of pine forest affected by mountain pine beetle outbreaks in British Columbia since 1910. Reduction of the area affected after the 2007 peak is due to a lack of available host trees and a harsher winter. Sources: Alfaro et al. (2010), Canadian Forest Service Forest Insect and Disease Survey, British Columbia Ministry of Forests and Range

The combination of biodiversity loss, climate change and habitat degradation can lead to the proliferation of forest fires, pests and disease. Forests are naturally dynamic systems, but their loss and degradation on a scale unprecedented in human history could exceed ecological thresholds. An ecological threshold is the point at which an abrupt change can occur in an ecosystem (Groffman et al. 2006). Such a change could bring about substantial degradation or even collapse of a (forest) ecosystem, with significant loss of biodiversity and the services it provides (Rockström et al. 2009, Thompson et al. 2009, Leadley et al. 2010, Vergara and Scholz 2010).

Predicting ecological thresholds is very difficult, as processes of change are influenced by multiple variables. However, new scientific evidence is emerging about signals that can help identify different thresholds in forest ecosystems (Biggs et al. 2009, Rockström et al. 2009). For example, reduced diversity among tree species and in stand age has made forests in western North America particularly vulnerable to pest outbreaks on mature pine. As warmer winters improved the over-wintering survival of the mountain pine beetle, an extraordinary pest outbreak occurred during the last decade with major ecological and economic consequences (**Box 2**).

Changes in the resilience of forest ecosystems can also threaten forest-based climate mitigation strategies (Thompson et al. 2009). For example, forests' climate mitigation benefits may be at risk if projects designed to sequester atmospheric carbon are affected by severe fires or pest outbreaks. Single-species carbon stocks with low biodiversity could be particularly vulnerable to stresses, as demonstrated by the mountain pine beetle outbreak. The ecological impact of this outbreak changed the net carbon balance of Canada's forests, which became a carbon source instead of a carbon sink, affecting the country's total carbon budget (Kurz et al. 2008). In the peak year, the direct impact of the mountain pine beetle outbreak in terms of CO_2 emissions was 20 megatonnes of carbon from the decay of dead trees and net changes in sequestration. These emissions were equivalent to 75 per cent of average annual direct forest fire emissions from all of Canada between 1959 and 1999 (Kurz et al. 2008). To mitigate such threats to forest-based climate mitigation strategies, forest management needs to be improved by promoting greater diversity in tree species and age class and by considering the possible impacts of climate change.

Approaches to biodiversity conservation

Common insights and principles that can improve forest biodiversity conservation in a variety of landscapes and land uses are emerging from research and practice (Brokerhoff et al. 2008, Gardner et al. 2009, Anand et al. 2010, Gilbert-Norton et al. 2010, Lindenmayer and Hunter 2010). They include better understanding the importance of landscape mosaics and forest remnants; connectivity across landscape gradients and between remnants; the variable responses of individual species to disturbances; and the roles of various forms of planted forests, including plantation forests, in biodiversity conservation. Better approaches to conceiving, planning and managing land use change are also envisaged or being implemented (Kanowski and Murray 2008, Franklin and Lindenmayer 2009, Pfund 2010). These approaches look beyond a narrow concentration on individual species and particular land uses to recognize interdependencies between landscape elements, and between ecosystems and human populations (Bond and Parr 2010). More integrated management approaches, adapted to both social and ecological processes, are being explored with regard to long-term biodiversity conservation (Grantham et al. 2009, Gardner et al. 2010). For example, many forest management strategies aimed at biodiversity conservation are consistent with strategies for climate change mitigation and adaptation, as well as with the objectives and practice of sustainable forestry more generally (Bauhus et al. 2009, Innes et al. 2009, Klenner et al. 2009, Thompson et al. 2009).

Ecosystem-based management considers the full array of interactions within an ecosystem, including human activity. Rather than managing a single forest in isolation, it accounts for these interactions across the landscape mosaic of multiple land uses (Gardner et al. 2009). Ecosystem-based management can therefore enhance biodiversity conservation in the context of broad-scale land-use change (Pfund 2010). It includes the maintenance of natural forests and of ecological functions and processes across multiple land uses (Gardner et al. 2009). The extent of natural forest maintained in a human-modified landscape primarily determines species richness (Anand et al. 2010). This is because these remnant forests—given adequate size and appropriate configuration—are refuges for highly sensitive species and play an important role in forming ecological corridors that facilitate species movement across fragmented landscapes (Crooks and Sanjayan 2006, Gilbert-Norton et al. 2010). For example, biodiversity conservation in Brazil's highly fragmented Mata Atlântica rainforest has been enhanced by improving its connectivity with biodiversity-friendly land uses such as agroforestry and secondary forests (Ribeiro et al. 2009, Tabarelli et al. 2010). Ecosystem-based management approaches have also been successfully applied to plantations (**Box 3**).

In addition, maintaining and restoring habitat and connectivity in the landscape matrix between protected forest areas is of fundamental importance to biodiversity conservation (Lamb

Mosaic of rainforest and plantations at the Veracel pulp mill and tree plantation in the state of Bahia, Brazil. *Credit: Lasse Arvidson, Stora Enso*

Box 3: New generation plantations

Intensively managed planted forests are highly productive plantations primarily intended to produce wood and fibre. There are around 25 million hectares of intensively managed planted forests worldwide, representing one-quarter of plantation forests and almost 0.2 per cent of global land area. They generally comprise tropical 'fastwood' plantations of acacia and eucalyptus, as well as temperate conifers. Many of the issues relevant to these forests also apply to the even larger area of tropical tree crops grown for non-wood products—coconut, oil palm and rubber (Kanowski and Murray 2008).

The New Generation Plantations Project led by WWF collects information and experience from tree plantations in a range of forest landscapes that are compatible with biodiversity conservation and human needs (NGPP 2010). This project is exploring how forest and plantation management can maintain and enhance ecosystem integrity and forest biodiversity (Neves Silva 2009). New approaches to plantation management can also enhance biodiversity at the stand level (Paquette and Messier 2010).

During the 1960s and 1970s, Brazil's Atlantic rainforest, Mata Atlântica, was deforested at an accelerated rate due to logging of valuable tree species for sawmilling and subsequent land clearance for cattle grazing. Management of a local pulp mill and tree plantation, which owns around 210 000 hectares in the region, has planted close to 91 000 hectares with eucalyptus on land previously used for cattle grazing, while more than 100 000 hectares are set aside for conservation. Eucalyptus is planted on plateaus, leaving valleys, river banks, steep slopes, and other areas with special characteristics reserved for environmental preservation. The area reserved for the rainforest is mainly regenerating naturally, but the most degraded parts are being restored through active planting of some 400 hectares of native species per year. The creation of forest corridors has enhanced connectivity between isolated remnants of the rainforest. At the end of 2009, over 3 500 hectares of rainforest had been restored (NGPP 2010).

At the landscape level, the plantations have had positive effects by stabilizing land use and reversing gradual forest degradation caused by cattle grazing. They have also made a significant contribution to biodiversity conservation by creating conditions for the protection and regeneration of the Atlantic rainforest.

et al. 2005, Franklin and Lindenmayer 2009). A meta-analysis of 89 restoration assessments, covering a wide range of ecosystem types, indicated that restoration increased biodiversity and the provision of ecosystem services such as regulation of water flow, particularly in the biodiversity-rich tropics (Benayas et al. 2009). However, it also highlighted the challenges involved in restoring degraded ecosystems and the decadal or greater timescales required. Such analyses have repeatedly demonstrated that it is preferable to avoid degradation and conserve forest biodiversity before restoration measures become necessary (TEEB 2009).

Adaptive management, too, has emerged as essential to forest biodiversity conservation, in part because it can enhance ecosystem resilience (Walker and Salt 2006, Nitschke and Innes 2008, Thompson et al. 2009). It uses a flexible, step-based approach to learn from experience, experimentation and monitoring (UNEP-WCMC 2010). An adaptive approach can help develop strategies that deliver ecological, economic and social benefits (PA 2009). Practitioners have found that, when its co-management dimensions are emphasized, this approach can be a pragmatic way to build consensus among multiple stakeholders in meeting forest management and biodiversity conservation goals (Innes et al. 2009, Maris and Béchet 2010). However, the pilot activities supporting most adaptive management initiatives for biodiversity conservation have often lacked the financial and human resources to replicate or scale up practices developed at the project level (Bille 2010). For adaptive management to be effective in forest biodiversity conservation on a larger scale, greater and more sustained investment in social and institutional capacity will be necessary.

To support and improve forest management practices, new tools, methods and practices are being developed to monitor biodiversity and increase stakeholder participation. For example, new technology and mapping systems have been used to guide forest conservation practices and inform policy (**Box 4**). More generally, it is now recognized that effective forest conservation and management require institutions and processes that incorporate multiple levels and forms of information and knowledge, and that build learning partnerships (Berkes 2007, Andersson and Ostrom 2008). In addition, implementing market-based mechanisms for climate change mitigation through forest conservation, such as reducing emissions from deforestation and forest degradation in developing countries (REDD+), require much better monitoring, reporting and verification systems than currently exist (Angelsen 2009). In response to these needs, new ways to generate, manage and share information and knowledge that can be used in forest conservation and management are emerging.

Box 4: Managing information for change

Forest management is being revolutionized by technologies that increase the speed at which vast amounts of spatial and temporal data can be analyzed and synthesized. Tools to enable near real-time monitoring of forests and carbon stocks are under development. An example is the Earth Engine platform launched by Google in 2010. This new technology platform is designed to improve access to satellite imagery, ground-sampling and other Earth observation data, and to provide computational resources for processing high-resolution data on a global scale that can help monitor deforestation and forest degradation. It also provides an open application framework that allows scientists to develop and run computer programs such as forest area change detection and biomass and carbon estimation (Google 2010). Although forest extent and carbon stocks can be monitored using these new tools, they will need to be complemented by on-the-ground monitoring to assess biodiversity.

In addition, a wide range of new techniques can support community-based participatory data collection using Geographic Information Systems (GIS). These techniques appear to offer a new and powerful way to include local groups in planning and decision-making. They are already being used throughout Africa, Asia and Latin America to engage local communities and assist with forest monitoring and management.

A recent Amazon Conservation Team project in the states of Pará and Amazonas in northern Brazil trained five indigenous groups to create cultural and land use maps of their territories. These maps include over 5 000 indigenous place names and other traditional designations and over 10 million hectares of land of cultural, natural and historical significance (Amazon Conservation Team 2010). The maps have been used in decision-making and the development of forest conservation strategies. This process has facilitated co-operation among stakeholders.

Members of the Tiriyó indigenous group and researchers in the Republic of Suriname. Participatory mapping can help indigenous groups make informed decisions about land use and forest conservation. *Credit: Amazon Conservation Team*

Giving full value to living forests

One of the greatest constraints on forest biodiversity conservation has been market failures, such as a lack of price signals and undervaluation of the multiple services provided by forests, meaning that forests may be considered to be 'worth more dead than alive' (Mooney 2000). Better recognition of the value of living forests' biodiversity and ecosystem services is one of the keys to better conservation outcomes. Not only is slowing the rate of deforestation central to biodiversity conservation and the protection of ecosystem services, but it is one of the quickest and most economical carbon abatement options (Prince's Rainforest Project 2009, Corbera et al. 2010). Stern (2007) estimated that it would cost only US$10-15 billion a year to halve the rate of deforestation by 2030. By comparison, the total value of forest product removals in 2005 was US$122 billion, not accounting for other values such as employment and services (FAO 2010). The extent of forest within protected areas has doubled during the past 20 years, but that level of progress has not been matched by financial investments (FAO 2010). This is particularly true in tropical developing countries that are rich in biodiversity, where funding for protected areas is 70 per cent below what is required for more effective conservation (TEEB 2010). Historically, official development assistance (ODA) has been the largest source of such funding. However, an important new source is market-based mechanisms, including eco-tourism, the sale of certified forest products, payments for ecosystem services, and biodiversity offsets (Crowe and ten Kate 2010). Payments for ecosystem services have gained importance as an approach that could potentially promote economic growth as well as financing biodiversity conservation (TEEB 2009) (**Figure 4**).

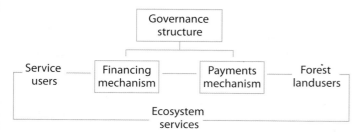

Figure 4: Most payments for ecosystem services schemes are characterized by voluntary transactions involving well-defined environmental services or forms of land use that are likely to secure those services (for example, food, fibre, water purification or recreational services). Through financing and payment mechanisms, service users pay forest land users for providing those services. *Source: Pagiola and Platais (2005)*

REDD+ is a new policy mechanism that adopts the payments for ecosystem services approach on a global scale. Its purpose is to reduce emissions from deforestation and forest degradation, while also generating financial flows from North to South. REDD+ has been facilitated by initiatives such as the Interim REDD+ Partnership (REDD+ Partnership 2010) and was endorsed at the UN Climate Change Conference in Cancún (UNFCCC 2010). Many scientists and practitioners believe REDD+ can deliver co-benefits additional to climate change mitigation, including forest biodiversity conservation (Angelsen 2009, Dickson and Osti 2010, Strassburg et al. 2010). Other stakeholders are concerned about the political and economic implications of market-based mechanisms and the possibility that REDD+ implementation arrangements could ignore the rights of indigenous and forest-dependent people to their territories and resources (GFC 2008, IIPFCC 2009, Phelps et al. 2010). Such concerns have been acknowledged in UNFCCC negotiations through recognition that environmental and social safeguards are needed with regard to REDD+ (UNFCCC 2009, Sikor et al. 2010). If successful, REDD+ could generate substantial revenues for conservation and sustainable forest management, as well as benefiting rural poverty reduction and improvement of rural livelihoods.

Maps from a study by Strassburg et al. (2010) illustrate the strong congruence between carbon stocks and biodiversity, especially in the case of forest ecosystems (**Figure 5**). This study and a review by Miles et al. (2010) suggest that synergies for co-benefits are considerable in many cases, but not in all. REDD+ with appropriate safeguards offers prospects for achieving biodiversity conservation goals in developing countries that have proved elusive since the 1992 Earth Summit. Experience with payments for ecosystem services provides guidance with regard to the development of REDD+ regimes that will deliver biodiversity co-benefits to a wide range of stakeholders (Wunder and Wertz-Kanounnikoff 2009). For example, the World Bank has announced a Wildlife Premium Market Initiative that will provide payments to the rural poor for protecting high biodiversity-value wildlife in forests within the context of a REDD+ mechanism (World Bank 2010).

Achieving the potential co-benefits of REDD+ at local level will depend on many elements: REDD+ design and financing arrangements; good governance structures and regulatory systems; an adaptive approach to the design and implementation of national and sub-national policies and strategies; agreement on and implementation of safeguards; clear guidance principles; effective capacity building; and adequate technology transfer (Angelsen 2009, Karousakis 2009, AWGLCA 2010, Busch et al. 2010, Dickson and Osti 2010).

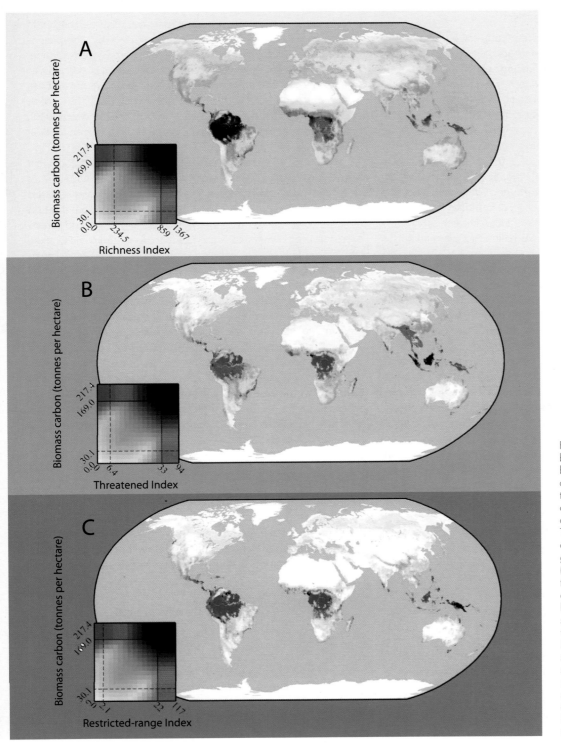

Figure 5: Global congruence between biomass carbon and biodiversity richness. Two-dimensional colour scales are used to display both the concentration of biomass carbon and biodiversity and the congruence between them. The intensity on the vertical blue axis represents above- and below-ground biomass carbon density (tonnes of carbon per hectare) and the intensity on the horizontal red axis the richness of the respective biodiversity index (number of species per cell). The maps show the global congruence between biomass carbon and (A) overall species richness, (B) threatened species richness, and (C) restricted-range species richness. Darker shading corresponds to higher concentrations of carbon and biodiversity. *Source: Strassburg et al. (2010)*

Trends in forest governance

Good forest governance is fundamental to achieving better biodiversity conservation outcomes (Agrawal et al. 2008, Sasaki and Putz 2009). Forest governance includes formal and informal institutions, as well as structures of authority and processes that determine to whom and how forests are allocated and how they are used and managed (Burris et al. 2005, Cashore 2009). Historically, forest governance has been characterized by state-centred, top-down approaches relying on command and control mechanisms that provide little recognition of the rights or interests of traditional owners (Agrawal et al. 2008). However, there have been strong trends away from this form of governance, driven by a realization of its limitations and the success of alternative models (Berkes 2007, Andersson and Ostrom 2008). Three critical trends in forest governance are described below. They are relevant to biodiversity conservation in a number of ways.

The first trend recognizes the persistence of the concession model of forest management. Under this model, governments allow private companies exclusive long-term resource rights to public forests in exchange for revenues. Concessions remain the dominant form of management of commercially valuable tropical forests (Agrawal et al. 2008). While well-designed and well-regulated concession agreements can promote sustainable forest management and reduce illegal logging, the converse is also true (Christy et al. 2007). Improving the governance of forest concessions therefore remains central to forest biodiversity conservation.

The second trend relates to greater decentralization in the management of the broader landscape. Governance at this level should take into account the socio-political context beyond local-level and forest-focused decision making (Lele et al. 2010). Decades of experience show that conserving biodiversity in protected areas depends crucially upon the inclusion of local people, particularly in countries with weak institutions where there are strong pressures on land (Sunderland et al. 2008, Sayer 2009). Local participation, empowerment and leadership are now widely acknowledged by practitioners as central to successful forest conservation initiatives (CBD 2009, Pfund 2010). Where local people are involved in this way, innovative governance can capitalize on opportunities provided by the participation of multiple actors in both policy design and implementation (Seppala et al. 2009).

The third trend relates to creating governance conditions for effectively implementing and benefiting from market-based mechanisms as a complement to—but not a substitute for—the role of the state (Gunningham 2009, Bille 2010, TEEB 2010). This is reflected in the 4th principle of the Ecosystem Approach framework of the Convention on Biological Diversity, which calls for aligning economic signals, sanctions and rewards with good ecosystem management (CBD 2009). A review by Bond et al. (2009) of lessons learned from payments for ecosystem services and REDD reported that the success of market-based instruments is strongly contingent on enabling economic, institutional, informational and cultural preconditions, such as clarity of land rights, functional systems to monitor compliance and apportion payments, and sufficient levels of trust and co-operation among stakeholders.

Each of these trends has the potential to work for or against forest biodiversity conservation. Evidence from a series of research studies indicates that the success of decentralized forest management regimes based on collective action is variable (Shackleton et al. 2010). Similarly, the increasing role of private sector forest ownership and management can have mixed results for conservation, ranging from highly enabling to greatly constraining (Lele et al. 2010, McDermott et al. 2010). There have also been challenges with regard to achieving the objectives of market-based instruments. An example is forest certification, which has had some success in supporting biodiversity conservation (Zagt et al. 2010) but mainly outside tropical forests (**Figure 6**). According to Cashore et al. (2006), the low uptake of tropical forest certification reflects poor forest governance and limited market demand for certified products. The importance of new forms of forest governance for forest biodiversity conservation is increasing, as experience with their implementation grows and as markets and society respond to public concern about deforestation, forest degradation and biodiversity loss.

Looking ahead

Loss of forest biodiversity can reduce the resilience of forests and leave them more vulnerable to mounting pressures, including climate change. Growing evidence suggests that biodiversity loss makes forest ecosystems more susceptible to existing pressures such as pests and allows outbreaks that cause substantial

Primary and secondary forests

Primary forests are natural forests that are undisturbed (directly) by humans (FAO 2005).

Secondary forests are forests that are regenerated largely through natural processes, following significant human or natural disturbance of the original forest vegetation (FAO 2005).

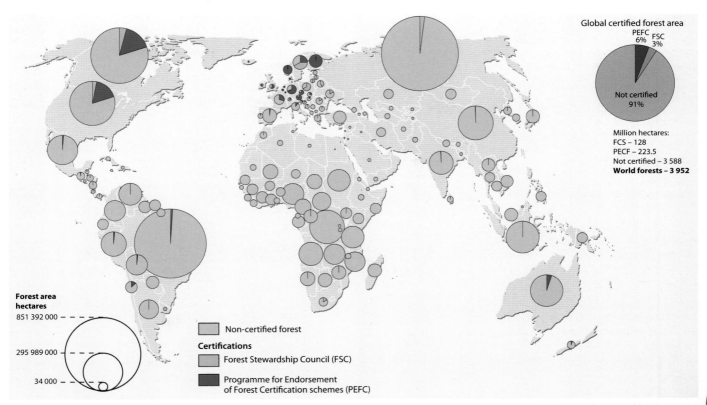

Forest area hectares
851 392 000
295 989 000
34 000

Non-certified forest

Certifications
Forest Stewardship Council (FSC)

Programme for Endorsement of Forest Certification schemes (PEFC)

Global certified forest area
PEFC 6%
FSC 3%
Not certified 91%

Million hectares:
FCS – 128
PECF – 223.5
Not certified – 3 588
World forests – 3 952

Figure 6: Global distribution of forest certification in 2009. Most certified forest areas are found in North America and Europe. Certification of biodiversity-rich tropical forests has so far been limited. *Source: Adapted from FAO (2009), FSC (2009), PEFC (2009), and UNEP/GRID-Arendal (2009)*

degradation or even ecosystem collapse. Degraded forests are less able to sustain and deliver the goods and services that society values and needs.

Primary forests, which have the highest biodiversity value, are the focus of the greatest biodiversity conservation efforts (FAO 2010). However, other forests—including managed and secondary forests and forests in remnant patches and corridors, on sites being restored and rehabilitated, and in agro-ecosystems or peri-urban landscapes—are also critical for biodiversity conservation. The value of these forests and their interdependencies are increasingly recognized in landscape approaches to biodiversity conservation.

Innovative and effective responses are necessary to meet the challenges of forest biodiversity conservation. The foundations for such responses have been established. Ecosystem-based approaches to forest management are fundamental to forest biodiversity conservation. They recognize the diversity of values and interests in forests, the need for people to participate in decisions about forests in order to enable more effective conservation outcomes, and the need to sustain these outcomes

in a landscape context. Similarly, adaptive management strategies focus on learning from the experience of all stakeholders to improve forest management and biodiversity conservation. Improved forest governance is also crucial. It can draw on a range of innovative market-based instruments and more community-based mechanisms. The emergence of REDD+ exemplifies the opportunities, but also the challenges, of using market-based instruments that can potentially deliver major biodiversity conservation benefits. New information technologies that improve monitoring and enhance science-based policy development are beginning to play a key role in conservation efforts.

Like the International Year of Biodiversity in 2010, the International Year of Forests in 2011 emphasizes the importance of forest biodiversity. Each illustrates a paradox. Whereas knowledge and understanding of biodiversity, and of its value, have never been greater, neither have the pressures on biodiversity been greater in human history than they are today. Conservation of forest biodiversity is fundamental to sustaining forests and people in a world adapting to climate change.

References

Agrawal, A., Chhatre, A. and Hardin, R. (2008). Changing Governance of the World's Forests. *Science*, 320, 1460-1462

Alfaro, R.I., Hantula, J., Carroll, A., Battisti, A., Fleming, R., Woods, A., Hennon, P.E., Lanfranco, D., Ramos, M., Müller, M., Lilja, A. and Francis, D. (2010). Forest Health in a Changing Environment. Chapter 7 in: Mery, G., Katila, P., Galloway, G., Alfaro, R., Kanninen, M., Lobovikov, M. and Varjo, J. (eds.), *Forests and Society – Responding to Global Drivers of Change*. International Union of Forest Research Organizations (IUFRO) World Series. METLA, Helsinki

Alkemade, R., van Oorschot, M., Miles, L., Nellemann, C., Bakkenes, M. and ten Brink, B. (2009). GLOBIO3: A Framework to Investigate Options for Reducing Global Terrestrial Biodiversity Loss. *Ecosystems*, 12, 374-390

Amazon Conservation Team (2010). Participatory Ethnographic Mapping: Mapping Indigenous Lands. Amazon Conservation Team, Arlington, Virginia. http://www.amazonteam.org/index.php/193/Participatory_Ethnographic_Mapping_Mapping_Indigenous_Lands

Anand, M.O., Krishnaswamy, J., Kumar, A. and Bali, A. (2010). Biodiversity conservation in human-dominated landscapes in the Western Ghats: Remnant forests matter. *Biological Conservation*, 143, 2363-2374

Andersson, K.P. and Ostrom, E. (2008). Analyzing decentralized resource regimes from a polycentric perspective. *Policy Sciences*, 41, 71-93

Angelsen, A. (ed.) (2009). *Realising REDD+*. Centre for International Forestry Research, Bogor

Asner, G.P., Knapp, D.E., Broadbent, E.N., Oliveira, P.J.C., Keller, M. and Silva, J.N. (2005). Selective Logging in the Brazilian Amazon. *Science*, 310, 480-482

AWGLCA (2010). *Report of the Ad Hoc Working Group on Long-term Cooperative Action under the Convention on its eighth session from 7 to 15 December 2009*. FCCC/AWGLCA/2009/17. Copenhagen

Bauhus, J., Puettmann, K. and Messier, C. (2009). Silviculture for old-growth attributes. *Forest Ecology and Management*, 258, 525-537

Benayas, J.M.R., Newton, A.C., Diaz, A. and Bullock, J.M. (2009). Enhancement of biodiversity and ecosystem services by ecological restoration: A meta-analysis. *Science*, 325, 1121-1124

Berkes, F. (2007). Community-based conservation in a globalized world. Proceedings of the National Academy of Sciences, 104, 15188-15193

Biggs, R., Carpenter, S.R.R. and Brock, W.A. (2009). Turning back from the brink: Detecting an impending regime shift in time to avert it. *Proceedings of the National Academy of Sciences*, 106, 826-831

Bille, R. (2010). Action without change? On the use and usefulness of pilot experiments in environmental management. *Veolia Environment*, 3, 1-6

Bond, I., Grieg-Gran, M., Wertz-Kanounnikoff, S., Hazlewood, P., Wunder, S. and Angelsen, A. (2009). *Incentives to sustain forest ecosystem services: A review and lessons for REDD*. International Institute for Environment and Development (IIED), London

Bond, W.J. and Parr, C.L. (2010). Beyond the forest edge: Ecology, diversity and conservation of the grassy biome. *Biological Conservation*, 143, 2395-2404

Brockerhoff, E., Jactel, H., Parrotta, J.A., Quine, C. and Sayer, J. (2008). Biodiversity and Planted Forests – Oxymoron or Opportunity? *Biodiversity and Conservation*, 17, 925-951

Burris, S., Drahos, P. and Shearing, C. (2005). Nodal governance. *Australian Journal of Legal Philosophy*, 30, 30-58

Busch, J., Godoy, F., Turner, W.R. and Harvey, C.A. (2010). Biodiversity co-benefits of reducing emissions from deforestation under alternative reference levels and levels of finance. *Conservation Letters*, No. doi: 10.1111/j.1755-263X.2010.00150.x

Carroll, A.L., Taylor, S.W., Régnière, J. and Safranyik, L. (2004). Effects of climate and climate change on the mountain pine beetle. In: Shore, T.L., Brooks, J.E. and Stone, J.E. (eds.), *Challenges and Solutions: Proceedings of the Mountain Pine Beetle Symposium*. Canadian Forest Service, Pacific Forestry Centre, Kelowna, British Columbia

Cashore, B. (2009). *Key Components of Good Forest Governance*. ASEAN Forests Clearing House Mechanism, ASEAN Secretariat, Jakarta

Cashore, B., Gale, F., Meidinger, E. and Newsom, D. (2006). Conclusion. In: Cashore, B., Gale, F., Meidinger, E. and Newsom, D. (eds.), *Confronting Sustainability: Forest Certification in Developing and Transitioning Countries*. Yale School of Forestry and Environmental Studies, New Haven

CBD (1992). Convention on Biological Diversity, Text and Annexes. The Interim Secretariat for the CBD, Geneva Executive Centre, Geneva

CBD (2009). Connecting Biodiversity and Climate Change Mitigation and Adaptation. Report of the Second Ad Hoc Technical Expert Group on Biodiversity and Climate Change. Secretariat of the Convention on Biological Diversity, Montreal

CBD (2010). *Global Biodiversity Outlook 3*. Secretariat of the Convention on Biological Diversity, Montreal

Christy, L., Di Leva, C., Lindsay, J. and Talla Takoukam P. (2007). *Forest Law and Sustainable Development: Addressing Contemporary Challenges Through Legal Reform*. World Bank Law, Justice, and Development Series. World Bank, Washington, D.C.

Corbera, E., Estrada, M. and Brown, K. (2010). Reducing greenhouse gas emissions from deforestation and forest degradation in developing countries: Revisiting the assumptions. *Climatic Change*, 100, 355-388

Crooks, K.R. and Sanjayan, M. (eds.) (2006). *Connectivity Conservation*. Conservation Biology 14. Cambridge

Crowe, M. and ten Kate, K. (2010). *Biodiversity offsets: Policy options for government*. Forest Trends, Washington, D.C.

DeFries, R.S., Rudel, T., Uriarte, M. and Hansen, M. (2010). Deforestation driven by urban population growth and agricultural trade in the twenty-first century. *Nature Geoscience*, 3, 178-181

Dickson, B. and Osti, M. (2010). *What are the ecosystem-derived benefits of REDD+ and why do they matter?* Multiple Benefits Series 1. UN-REDD Programme, Nairobi

FAO (2000). *Global Forest Resources Assessment 2000*. Food and Agriculture Organization of the United Nations, Rome

FAO (2005). *Global Forest Resources Assessment Update. 2005 Terms and Definitions*. Forest Resources Assessment Working Paper 83. Food and Agriculture Organization of the United Nations, Rome

FAO (2007). *The State of the World's Forests 2007*. Food and Agriculture Organization of the United Nations, Rome

FAO (2009a). *The State of the World's Forests 2009*. Food and Agriculture Organization of the United Nations, Rome

FAO (2009b). Forests and the global economy: 10 million new jobs. Press release. Food and Agriculture Organization of the United Nations, Rome

FAO (2010). *Global Forest Resources Assessment 2010*. Food and Agriculture Organization of the United Nations, Rome

Franklin, J. and Lindenmayer, D. (2009). Importance of matrix habitats in maintaining biological diversity. *Proceedings of the National Academy of Sciences*, 106(2), 349-350

FSC (2009). *Annual Report 2009*. Forest Stewardship Council, Bonn

Gardner, T.A., Barlow, J., Chazdon, R.L., Ewers, R., Harvey, C.A., Peres, C.A. and Sodhi, N.S. (2009). Prospects for tropical forest biodiversity in a human-modified world. *Ecology Letters*, 12, 561-582

Gardner, T.A., Barlow, J., Sodhi, N.S. and Peres, C.A. (2010). A multi-region assessment of tropical forest biodiversity in a human-modified world. *Biological Conservation*, 143(10), 2293-2300

GFC (2008). *Life as commerce: The impact of market-based conservation on Indigenous Peoples, local communities and women*. Global Forest Coalition, Asunción, Paraguay. http://www.globalforestcoalition.org/img/userpics/File/publications/LIFE-AS-COMMERCE2008.pdf

Gilbert-Norton, L., Wilson, R., Stevens, J.R. and Beard, K.H. (2010). A meta-analytic review of corridor effectiveness. *Conservation Biology*, 24, 660-668

Google (2010). The Earth Engine. Google.org. http://googleblog.blogspot.com/2009/12/seeing-forest-through-cloud.html

Grantham, H.S., Bode, M., McDonald-Madden, E., Game, E.T., Knight, A.T. and Possingham, H.P. (2009). Effective conservation planning requires learning and adaptation. *Frontiers in Ecology and the Environment*, 8, 431-437

Groffman, P.M., Baron, J.S., Blett, T., Gold, A.J., Goodman, I., Gunderson, L.H., Levinson, B.M., Palmer, M.A., Paerl, H.W., Peterson, G.D., LeRoy Poff, N., Rejeski, D.W., Reynolds, J.F., Turner, M.G., Weathers, K.C. and Wiens, J. (2006). Ecological Thresholds: The Key to Successful Environmental Management or an Important Concept with No Practical Application? *Ecosystems*, 9, 1-13

Gunningham, N. (2009). Environment law, regulation and governance: Shifting architectures. *Journal of Environmental Law*, 21, 179-212

Haines-Young, R. and Potschin, M. (2009). The links between biodiversity, ecosystem services and human well-being. In: Raffaelli, D. and Frid, C. (eds.), *Ecosystem ecology: A new synthesis. BES Ecological Reviews Series*. Cambridge University Press, Cambridge

IIPFCC (2009). Statement on Shared Vision under AWG LCA, Copenhagen, 7 December 2009. International Indigenous Peoples' Forum on Climate Change. http://indigenouspeoplesissues.com

Innes, J., Joyce, L., Kellomaki, M., Louman, B., Ogden, A., Parrotta, J. and Thompson, I. (2009). Management for adaptation. Chapter 6 in: Seppala, R., Buck, A. and Katila, P. (eds.), *Adaptation of forests and people to climate change*. IUFRO World Series 22. International Union of Forest Research Organizations, Vienna

IUCN (2010). *Plants under pressure – a global assessment. The first report of the IUCN Sampled Red List Index for Plants*. Royal Botanic Gardens, Kew, UK, Natural History Museum, London, and International Union for Conservation of Nature

Kanowski, P. and Murray. H. (2008). *Intensively Managed Planted Forests. Toward best practice*. The Forests Dialogue, TFD Secretariat, New Haven

Karousakis, K. (2009). *Promoting Biodiversity Co-Benefits in REDD*. Organisation for Economic Co-operation and Development, Environment Working Papers. OECD, Paris

Klenner, W., Arsenault, A., Brockerhoff, E.G. and Vyse, A. (2009). Biodiversity in forest ecosystems and landscapes: A conference to discuss future directions in biodiversity management for sustainable forestry. *Forest Ecology and Management*, 258, S1-S4

Kurz, W.A., Dymond, C.C., Stinson, G., Rampley, G.J., Neilson, E.T., Carroll, A.L., Ebata, T. and Safranyik, L. (2008). Mountain pine beetle and forest carbon: Feedback to climate change. *Nature*, 452, 987-990

Lamb, D., Erskine, P. and Parrotta, J.A. (2005). Restoration of degraded tropical forest landscapes. *Science*, 310, 1628-1632

Leadley, P., Pereira, H.M., Alkemade, R., Fernandez-Manjarrés, J.F., Proença, V., Scharlemann, J.P.W. and Walpole, M.J. (2010). *Biodiversity Scenarios: Projections of 21st century change in biodiversity and associated ecosystem services*. Secretariat of the Convention on Biological Diversity, Montreal

Lele, S., Wilshusen, P., Brockington, D., Seidler, R. and Bawa, K. (2010). Beyond exclusion: Alternative approaches to biodiversity conservation in the developing tropics. *Current Opinion in Environmental Sustainability*, 2, 94-100

Lindenmayer, D., Fischer, J., Felton, A., Crane, M., Michael, D., Macgregor, C., Montague-Drake, R., Manning, A. and Hobbs, R. (2008). Novel ecosystems resulting from landscape transformation create dilemmas for modern conservation practice. *Conservation Letters*, 1(3), 129-135

Lindenmayer, D. and Hunter, M. (2010). Some Guiding Concepts for Conservation Biology. *Conservation Biology*, 24, 1459-1468

MA (2005a). *Ecosystems and Human Well-being: Biodiversity Synthesis*. Millennium Ecosystem Assessment. Island Press, Washington, D.C.

MA (2005b). *Ecosystems and Human Well-being: Synthesis*. Millennium Ecosystem Assessment. Island Press, Washington, D.C.

Malhi, Y., Aragao, L.E.O.C., Galbraith, D., Huntingford, C., Fisher, R., Zelazowski, P., Sitch, S., McSweeney, C. and Meir, P. (2009). Exploring the likelihood and mechanism of a climate-change induced dieback of the Amazon rainforest. *Proceedings of the National Academy of Sciences*, 106, 20610-20615

Maris, V., and Béchet, A. (2010). From adaptive management to adjustive management: A pragmatic account of biodiversity values. *Conservation Biology*, 24, 966-973

Menéndez, R., González, A., Hill, J.K., Braschler, B., Willis, S.G., Collingham, Y., Fox, R., Roy, D.B. and Thomas, C.D. (2006). Species richness changes lag behind climate change. *Proceedings of the Royal Society B*, 273(1593), 1465-1470

Midgley, G.F., Bond, J., Kapos, V., Ravilious, C., Scharlemann, J.P.W. and Woodward, F.I. (2010). Terrestrial carbon stocks and biodiversity: Key knowledge gaps and some policy implications. *Current Opinion in Environmental Sustainability*, 2, 264-270

Miles, L., Dunning, E., Doswald, N. and Osti, M. (2010). *A safer bet for REDD+: Review of the evidence on the relationship between biodiversity and the resilience of forest carbon stocks*. Working Paper v.2. Multiple Benefits Series 10. Prepared on behalf of the UN-REDD Programme. UNEP World Conservation Monitoring Centre, Cambridge

Mooney, H. (2000). Worth more dead than alive. *Nature*, 403, 593-594

Nellemann, C. and Corcoran, E. (eds). (2010). *Dead Planet, Living Planet – Biodiversity and Ecosystem Restoration for Sustainable Development*. A Rapid Response Assessment. United Nations Environment Programme, UNEP/GRID-Arendal, Arendal

Nellemann, C., MacDevette, M., Eickhout, B., Svihus, B., Prins, A.G. and Kaltenborn, B.P. (eds). (2009). *The Environmental Food Crisis*. A UNEP Rapid Response Assessment. United Nations Environment Programme, UNEP/GRID-Arendal, Arendal

Neves Silva, L. (2009). *Ecosystem integrity and forest plantations*. NGPP Ecosystem Integrity Technical Paper, WWF International

NGPP (2010). Case study 8/ Conserving the Atlantic Rainforest in Brazil. New Generation Plantations Project. http://newgenerationplantations.com/showcase.html

Nitschke, C.R. and Innes, J.L. (2008). Integrating climate change into forest management in South-Central British Columbia: An assessment of landscape vulnerability and development of a climate-smart framework. *Forest Ecology and Management*, 256, 313-327

PA (2009). *The Economic Cost of Climate Change in Africa*. Practical Action Consulting, Pan-African Climate Justice Alliance, Nairobi

Pagiola, S., Platais, G. (2005). Introduction to Payments for Environmental Services. Presentation. World Bank, Washington. D.C.

Paquette, A. and Messier, C. (2010) The role of plantations in managing the world's forests in the Anthropocene. *Frontiers in Ecology and the Environment*, 8, 27-34

PEFC (2009). PEFC Annual Review 2009. Programme for the Endorsement of Forest Certification, Geneva

Pfund, J.L. (2010). Landscape-scale research for conservation and development in the tropics: Fighting persisting challenges. *Current Opinion in Environmental Sustainability*, 2 (1-2), 117-126

Phelps, J., Webb, E.L. and Agrawal, A. (2010). Does REDD+ Threaten to Recentralize Forest Governance? *Science*, 328, 312-313

Prince's Rainforest Project (2009). An emergency package for tropical forests. Prince's Rainforest Project, London. http://www.rainforestsos.org/

Raffa, K.F., Aukema, B.H., Bentz, B.J., Carroll, A.L., Hicke, J.A., Turner, M.G. and Romme, W.H. (2008). Cross-scale drivers of natural disturbances prone to anthropogenic amplification: The dynamics of bark beetle eruptions. *Bioscience*, 58(6), 501-517

Rayner, J., Buck, A. and Katila, P. (eds.) (2010). *Embracing complexity: Meeting the challenges of international forest governance*. IUFRO World Series, 28. International Union of Forest Research Organizations, Vienna

REDD+ Partnership (2010). About the REDD+ Partnership. http://reddpluspartnership.org

Ribeiro, M.C., Metzger, J.P., Martensen, A.C., Ponzoni, F.J. and Hirota, M.M. (2009). The Brazilian Atlantic forest: How much is left, and how is the remaining forest distributed? Implications for conservation. *Biological Conservation*, 142, 1141-1153

Rockström, J., Steffen, W., Noone, K., Persson, Å., Chapin, F.S., Lambin, E., Lenton, T.M., Scheffer, M., Folke, C., Schellnhuber, H., Nykvist, B., De Wit, C.A., Hughes, T., van der Leeuw, S., Rodhe, H., Sörlin, S., Snyder, P.K., Costanza, R., Svedin, U., Falkenmark, M., Karlberg, L., Corell, R.W., Fabry, V.J., Hansen, J., Walker, B., Liverman, D., Richardson, K., Crutzen, P. and Foley, J. (2009). Planetary boundaries: Exploring the safe operating space for humanity. *Ecology and Society*, 14(2), 32

Safranyik, L. and Carroll, A.L. (2006). The biology and epidemiology of the mountain pine beetle in lodgepole pine forests. In: Safranyik, L. and Wilson, B. (eds.), *The Mountain Pine Beetle: A Synthesis of its Biology, Management and Impacts on Lodgepole Pine*. Natural Resources Canada, Canadian Forest Service, Pacific Forestry Centre, Victoria

Sasaki, N. and Putz, F.E. (2009). Critical need for new definitions of "forest" and "forest degradation" in global climate change agreements. *Conservation Letters*, 2, 226-232

Sayer, J. (2009). Reconciling Conservation and Development: Are Landscapes the Answer? *Biotropica*, 41(6), 649-652

Schmitt, C.B., Burgess, N.D., Coad, L., Belokurov, A., Besançon, C., Boisrobert, L., Campbell, A., Fish, L., Gliddon, D., Humphries, K., Kapos, V., Loucks, C., Lysenko, I., Miles, L., Mills, C., Minnemeyer, S., Pistorius, T., Ravilious, C., Steininger, M. and Winkel, G. (2009). Global analysis of the protection status of the world's forests. *Biological Conservation*, 142(10), 2122-2130

Schulze, C.H., Waltert, M., Kessler, P.J.A., Pitopang, R., Veddeler, D., Mühlenberg, M., Gradstein, S.R., Leuschner, C., Steffan-Dewenter, I. and Tscharntke, T. (2004). Biodiversity indicator groups of tropical land-use systems: Comparing plants, birds, and insects. *Ecological Applications*, 14,1321-1333

Seppala, R., Buck, A. and Katila, P. (2009). Executive summary and key message: *Adaptation of forests and people to climate change: A global assessment report*. IUFRO World Series 22. International Union of Forest Research Organizations, Vienna

Shackleton, C.M., Willis, T.J., Brown, K. and Polunin, N.V.C. (2010). Reflecting on the next generation of models for community-based natural resources management. *Environmental Conservation*, 37, 1-4

Sikor, T., Stahl, J., Enters, T., Ribot, J.C., Singh, N., Sunderlin, W.D. and Wollenberg, L. (2010). REDD-plus, forest people's rights and nested climate governance. *Global Environmental Change*, 20, 423-425

Slingenberg, A., Braat, L., van der Windt, H., Rademaekers, K., Eichler, L. and Turner, K. (2009). *Study on understanding the causes of biodiversity loss and the policy assessment framework*. European Commission Directorate-General for Environment. ECORYS Nederland BV, Rotterdam

Stern, N. (2007). *The Economics of Climate Change*. Cambridge University Press, Cambridge

Strassburg, B.B.N., Kelly, A., Balmford, A., Davies, R.G., Gibbs, H.K, Lovett, J., Miles, L., Orme, C.D.L., Price, J., Turner, R.K. and Rodrigues, A.S.L. (2010). Global congruence of carbon storage and biodiversity in terrestrial ecosystems. *Conservation Letters*, 3(2), 98-105

Sunderland, T., Ehringhaus, C. and Campbell, B. (2008). Conservation and development in tropical forest landscapes: A time to face the trade-offs? *Environmental Conservation*, 34(4), 276-279

Tabarelli, M., Aguiar, A.V., Ribeiro, M.C., Metzger, J.P. and Peres, C.A. (2010). Prospects for biodiversity conservation in the Atlantic Forest: Lessons from ageing human-modified landscapes. *Biological Conservation*, 143, 2328-2340

Taylor, S.W. and Carroll, A.L. (2004). Disturbance, forest age dynamics and mountain pine beetle outbreaks in BC: A historical perspective. In: Shore, T.L., Brooks, J.E. and Stone, J.E. (eds.), *Challenges and Solutions: Proceedings of the Mountain Pine Beetle Symposium*. Canadian Forest Service, Pacific Forestry Centre, Kelowna

Taylor, S.W., Carroll, A.L., Alfaro, R.I. and Safranyik, L. (2006). Forest, climate and mountain pine beetle dynamics. In: Safranyik, L. and Wilson, B. (eds.), *The Mountain Pine Beetle: A Synthesis of its Biology, Management and Impacts on Lodgepole Pine*. Natural Resources Canada, Canadian Forest Service, Pacific Forestry Centre, Victoria

TEEB (2009). Report for National and International Policy Makers. The Economics of Ecosystems and Biodiversity. http://www.teebweb.org/ForPolicymakers/tabid/1019/Default.aspx

TEEB (2010). TEEB for Local and Regional Policy Makers. The Economics of Eco-systems and Biodiversity. http://www.teebweb.org/ForLocalandRegionalPolicy/tabid/1020/Default.aspx

Thompson, I., Mackey, B., McNulty, S. and Mosseler, A. (2009). *Forest Resilience, Biodiversity, and Climate Change. A synthesis of the biodiversity/resilience/stability relationship in forest ecosystems*. Secretariat of the Convention on Biological Diversity, Montreal

UNEP (2007). *Global Environment Outlook 4*. United Nations Environment Programme, Nairobi

UNEP/GRID-Arendal (2009). Vital Forest Graphics. http://maps.grida.no/go/collection/vital-forest-graphics

UNEP-WCMC (2009). Framing the flow: Innovative approaches to understand, protect and value ecosystem services across linked habitats. Silvestri, S. and Kershaw, F. (eds.). United Nations Environment Programme and World Conservation Monitoring Centre, Cambridge

UNFCCC (2009). Report of the Conference of the Parties on its fifteenth session, held in Copenhagen from 7 to 19 December 2009. Addendum. Part Two: Action taken by the Conference of the Parties at its fifteenth session. Decision 4/CP.15 Methodological guidance for activities relating to reducing emissions from deforestation and forest degradation and the role of conservation, sustainable management of forests and enhancement of forest carbon stocks in developing countries. United Nations Framework Convention on Climate Change, Bonn. http://unfccc.int/resource/docs/2009/cop15/eng/11a01.pdf

UNFCCC (2010). Outcome of the Ad Hoc Working Group on long-term Cooperative Action under the Convention. United Nations Framework Convention on Climate Change. http://unfccc.int/meetings/cop_16/items/5571.php

Vergara, W. and Scholz, S.M. (2010). *Assessment of the risk of Amazon dieback*. World Bank Studies. World Bank, Washington, D.C.

Vos, C., Berry, P., Opdam, P., Baveco, H., Nijhor, B., O'Hanley, J., Bell, C. and Kuipers, H. (2008). Adapting landscapes to climate change: Examples of climate-proof ecosystem networks and priority adaptation zones. *Journal of Applied Ecology*, 45, 1722-1731

Walker, B. and Salt, D. (2006). Resilience thinking: Sustaining ecosystems and people in a changing world. Island Press, Washington, D.C.

World Bank (2010). Remarks for Opening Plenary of the High Level Segment – COP10, Nagoya, Japan. http://web.worldbank.org/WBSITE/EXTERNAL/NEWS/0,,contentMDK:22745069~pagePK:34370~piPK:34424~theSitePK:4607,00.html

World Bank (2004). Sustaining Forests: A Development Strategy. World Bank, Washington, D.C.

Wunder, S. and Wertz-Kanounnikoff, S. (2009). Payments for ecosystem services: A new way of conserving biodiversity in forests. *Journal of Sustainable Forestry*, 28, 576-596

Zagt, R.J., Sheil, D. and Putz, F.E. (2010). Biodiversity conservation in certified forests: An overview. In: Sheil, D., Putz, F.E. and Zagt, R.J. (eds.), *Biodiversity conservation in certified forests*. ETFRN News No. 51. Tropenbos, Wageningen

The capacity of wind power installations increased by 35.8 gigawatts in 2010, a 22.5 per cent increase over 2009. New capacity added in 2010 represented investments worth US$65 billion. The total installed wind energy capacity is 194.4 gigawatt. *Source: GWEC (2011); Credit: Tom Corser*

Key Environmental Indicators

Indicators help to assess the overall outcomes of complex interactions between people and the environment. The latest environmental data and trends show progress in addressing stratospheric ozone depletion, the uptake of renewable energy technologies, and the increasing use of environmental certification schemes. Global carbon dioxide emissions are still rising. Pressures on ecosystems from natural resource use persist, with notable impacts in terms of biodiversity loss.

Indicators can help tell us if problems are getting better or worse and if policy measures appear to be having an effect. For example, the rate of melting of mountain glaciers tells us something about atmospheric warming, while reduced production of ozone depleting substances indicates that countries are successfully phasing them out. However, indicators are no more than that—they indicate trends or report on the state of a single environmental component such as forest cover. Indicators do not explain underlying causes, nor does a lack of significant change

mean that no efforts have been made to address a problem. However, indicators can point out where further examination is needed.

Regular indicator-based assessments continue to be pivotal for presenting the bigger picture in regard to progress made towards achieving environmental sustainability. Every five years, the UNEP Global Environment Outlook (GEO) takes a comprehensive look at the state of and trends in the environment.

An overview of major global and regional trends is presented in this section, illustrated with 20 specially prepared graphics. According to the overall picture that emerges, in a few areas—such as stratospheric ozone depletion, renewable energy use and forest certification—there are signs of progress. Nevertheless, many pressures on the environment are continuing to persist. The rapid loss of both terrestrial and marine biodiversity is of particular concern, as highlighted in a number of recent publications (Butchard et al. 2010, SCBD 2010).

As in the case of the MDGs, this type of `global environmental snapshot' can serve to draw attention to the most pressing issues and monitor major trends in areas such as climate change, freshwater quality, use of natural resources, biodiversity loss and environmental governance. Poor availability of environmental data—especially from developing countries—is one of the major constraints on identifying global environmental trends.

Indicators are measures—generally quantitative—that can be used to illustrate and communicate complex phenomena in a simple way, including trends and progress over time (EEA 2005).

Index is a composite of several indicators.

Data source refers to the organization which prepared and provided the data.

MDG indicator An indicator that is included in the suite of indicators to track progress towards achieving the Millennium Development Goals (MDGs).

Depletion of the ozone layer

Since the establishment of the Montreal Protocol in the late 1980s, the world has succesfully phased out human-made ozone depleting substances (**Figure 1**). Although the problem of stratospheric ozone depletion is often seen as more or less controlled, production and consumption of certain ozone depleting substances continues through the substitution of substances such as hydrochlorofluorocarbons (HCFCs) as well as through permissions or exemptions, such as those for use of methyl bromide in agriculture. Illegal use of certain substances and of existing stockpiles is also an issue.

Consumption of ozone depleting substances

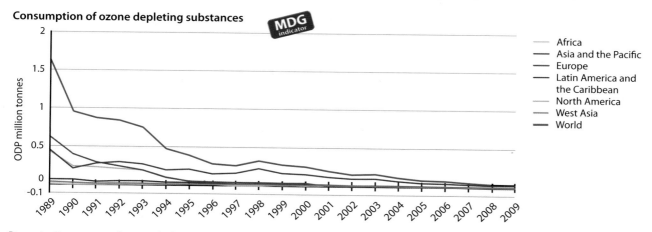

Legend:
- Africa
- Asia and the Pacific
- Europe
- Latin America and the Caribbean
- North America
- West Asia
- World

Figure 1: Consumption of ozone depleting substances expressed as million tonnes of ozone depletion potential (ODP), 1989-2009. ODP is a number that refers to the amount of ozone depletion caused by a chemical substance. Consumption of ozone depleting substances has largely been reduced in the past 20 years. *Data source: GEO Data Portal, compiled from the UNEP Secretariat for the Vienna Convention and the Montreal Protocol (UNEP 2010)*

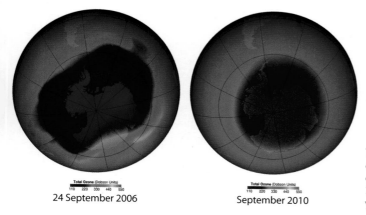

24 September 2006   September 2010

The largest ozone hole over the Antarctic since measurements began occurred in September 2006. It is estimated that by 2015 the width of the ozone hole will have been reduced by 1 million square kilometres out of 25 million square kilometres. Complete recovery is not expected until the year 2050 or later. *Source: NOAA (2010)*

Climate change

Carbon dioxide (CO_2) is one of the main anthropogenic greenhouse gases responsible for climate change. Globally, total CO_2 emissions continue to increase although regional differences are apparent (**Figure 2**). Emissions per capita vary greatly by region (**Figure 3**). While the climate negotiations have focused heavily on CO_2 emissions, the role of some common air pollutants as climate forcers is becoming clearer. Black carbon or soot is an important contributor to global warming. This pollutant, measured in terms of levels of particulate matter (**Figure 4**), is also a major health concern. Fine suspended particulates of 10 micrometres or less in diameter (PM_{10}) are capable of penetrating deep into the respiratory tract.

Carbon dioxide emissions

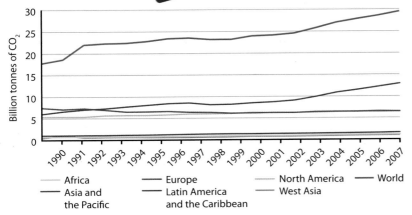

Figure 2: Carbon dioxide emissions from solid fuel consumption, expressed in billions of tonnes of CO_2, 1989-2007. Although emissions from fossil fuel consumption are stabilizing in Europe and North America, they are increasing in Asia and the Pacific. *Data sources: GEO Data Portal, compiled from the Carbon Dioxide Information Analysis Center (CDIAC), Boden et al. (2010)*

Carbon dioxide emission per capita

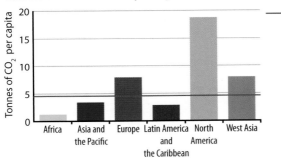

Figure 3: The latest data available on CO_2 emissions per capita, from 2007, show that there are large differences between regions. Emissions per capita are lowest in Africa. Those in North America, Europe and West Asia are well above the 2007 global average of 4.4 tonnes. *Data source: GEO Data Portal, compiled from the Carbon Dioxide Information Analysis Center (CDIAC), Boden et al. (2010)*

Concentration of particulate matter (PM_10)

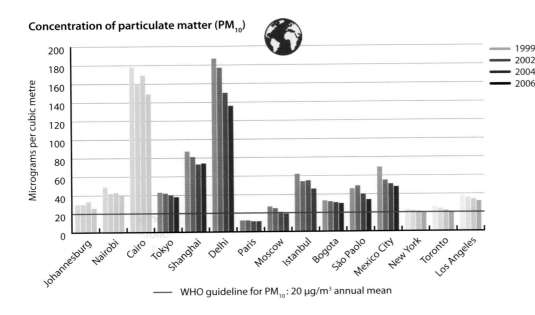

Figure 4: Estimated concentrations of particulate matter 10 micrometres or less in size (PM_10) per cubic metre in selected cities. These estimates represent average annual exposure to outdoor particulate matter by urban residents away from 'hotspots' such as industrial areas or transport corridors. In many parts of the world, air quality in major cities exceeds the WHO guideline of 20 µg/m³. *Data source: GEO Data Portal, compiled from the World Bank (2006, 2008 and 2010), Pandey et al. (2006)*

Renewable energy supply index

— Solar photovoltaics
— Solar thermal
— Wind
— Biofuels - biogasoline
       and biodiesel

Index (1990 = 100)

52 500
50 000
47 500
45 000
42 500
40 000
37 500
35 000
32 500
30 000
27 500
25 000
22 500
20 000
17 500
15 000
12 500
10 000
7 500
5 000
2 500
0

1990 1992 1994 1996 1998 2000 2002 2004 2006 2008

Both CO_2 and black carbon emissions result largely from fossil fuel combustion. The search for renewable energy is therefore fundamental for transitioning towards a greener economy (**Figure 5**). To track the effects of emissions already released and atmospheric processes under way as a result of past and current contributions, one of the key indicators used is the ice thickness change, or mass balance, of glaciers (**Figure 6**).

Mountain glacier mass balance

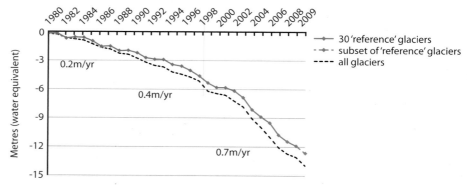

1980 1982 1984 1986 1988 1990 1992 1994 1996 1998 2000 2002 2004 2006 2008 2009

Metres (water equivalent)

0
-3
-6
-9
-12
-15

0.2m/yr
0.4m/yr
0.7m/yr

→ 30 'reference' glaciers
-◆- subset of 'reference' glaciers
--- all glaciers

Figure 6: Cumulative loss of ice thickness in mountain glaciers in metres of water equivalent, 1980-2009. Over the past three decades, the global average of available measurements shows a strong ice loss which has accelerated to 0.7 metre water equivalent during the past decade. *Data source: World Glacier Monitoring Service (WGMS 2010)*

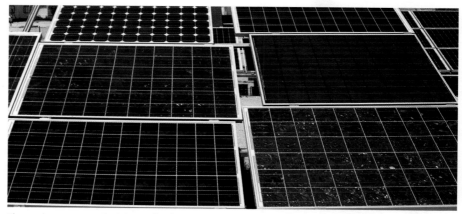

Photovoltaic array at the National Solar Energy Center, Jacob Blaustein Institutes for Desert Research, in the Negev Desert of Israel. *Credit: David Shankbone*

Figure 5: Renewable energy supply index (1990=100), 1990-2008. Although use of renewable energy is still modest compared to that of fossil fuels, at 13 per cent in 2008, recent increases are significant. Use of solar energy, particularly photovoltaics, has grown exponentially over the last years. Global use of other forms of renewable energy also continue to increase, with the exception of energy generated from tide, waves and the ocean. *Data source: GEO Data Portal, compiled from the International Energy Agency (IEA 2010)*

Natural resource use

Natural resources provide a livelihood for billions of people and are the basis of large parts of countries' economies. Sustainable use is essential to ensure the long-term availability of living resources such as forests and fish. Scientists have repeatedly expressed concern about the depletion of fish stocks (**Figure 7**), particularly in regard to heavily fished commercial species such as tuna (**Figure 8**).

Annual marine fish catch

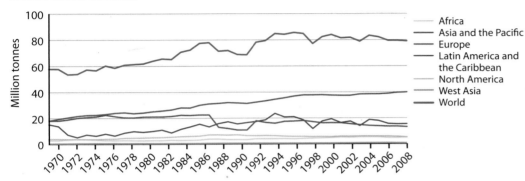

Africa
Asia and the Pacific
Europe
Latin America and the Caribbean
North America
West Asia
World

Figure 7: Annual marine fish catch in millions of tonnes, 1969-2008. Depletion of marine fish stocks is one of the most pressing environmental issues. With a global marine fish catch of approximately 80 million tonnes per year, pressure on marine ecosystems as a result of the exploitation of commercial fish species remains high. *Data source: GEO Data Portal, compiled from the Food and Agriculture Organization of the United Nations (FAO 2010a)*

More than two-thirds of tuna is caught in the Pacific Ocean. The Indian Ocean contributes more than the Atlantic and the Mediterranean Sea combined (20.4 and 9.5 per cent, respectively, in 2008). *Credit: National Atmospheric and Oceanographic Administration (NOAA)*

Global tuna catches

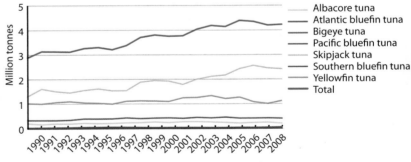

Albacore tuna
Atlantic bluefin tuna
Bigeye tuna
Pacific bluefin tuna
Skipjack tuna
Southern bluefin tuna
Yellowfin tuna
Total

Figure 8: Global catches of tuna and tuna-like species, 1989-2008. Economically important fish such as tuna are traded worldwide. Global production has increased from less than 0.6 million tonnes in 1950 to over 4 million tonnes today. A number of tuna species are overexploited. Although such deterioration could eventually lead to reduced catches, countries have been unable to come to an agreement on limiting trade in certain species. *Data source: GEO Data Portal, compiled from the Food and Agriculture Organization of the United Nations (FAO 2010a)*

Forest cover change (**Figure 9**) and the rate of harvesting of roundwood (**Figure 10**) are important indicators of the state of land ecosystems. While the extent of forest cover alone provides only limited information about forest biodiversity, afforestation efforts throughout the world have begun to show results and are building up carbon stock. Voluntary forest certification schemes, such as that established by the Forest Stewardship Council, take other ecosystem services into account (**Figure 11**). However, the impact of such schemes can be difficult to ascertain.

Proportion of land area covered by forest

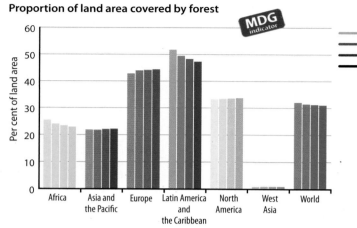

Figure 9: Proportion of land area covered by forest. Although the extent of forests is decreasing globally, there have been steady increases in Asia and the Pacific, Europe and North America. *Data source: GEO Data Portal, compiled from the Food and Agriculture Organization of the United Nations (FAO 2010b and c)*

Ratio of roundwood production and growing stock in forests

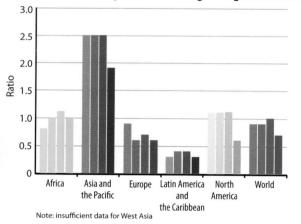

Note: insufficient data for West Asia

Figure 10: Forest harvest rates expressed as the ratio of roundwood production and growing stock in forests. After decades of increases, harvesting of roundwood from forests appears to have levelled off in recent years. In Asia and the Pacific roundwood production is very high and exceeds growth of forest stock. *Data source: GEO Data Portal, compiled from the Food and Agriculture Organization of the United Nations: FAO (2005) for 1990, 2000 and 2005; FAO (2010b) for 2010*

Figure 11: Total forest area certified by the Forest Stewardship Council (FSC), 2001-2010. The amount of forest certified with the FSC label is still modest in developing countries, but is growing rapidly in nothern regions. Globally, FSC certified forest represents 3.4 per cent of all forest area. FSC certification of a forest site means that an independent evaluation by an FSC accredited certification body has found that its management conforms to the internationally recognized FSC Principles and Criteria of Forest Stewardship. *Data source: GEO Data Portal, compiled from Forest Stewardship Council (FSC 2010)*

Forest area FSC-certified

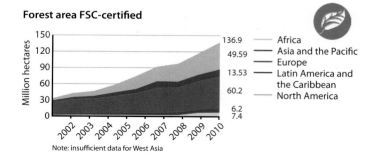

Note: insufficient data for West Asia

Biodiversity loss

In 2002, the world community established the target of significantly reducing biodiversity loss by 2010. Although this target was not met, a spotlight was focused on data insufficiency and the importance of biodiversity monitoring to measure results. Citizens and NGOs play a major monitoring role and are forming partnerships to undertake scientific and other joint activities, with the International Union for Conservation of Nature (IUCN) leading efforts in regard to threatened species (**Figure 12**). The UNEP World Conservation Monitoring Centre tracks, in collaboration with IUCN, the establishment of protected areas, a major policy response to help conserve biodiversity (**Figure 13**).

Threatened species index

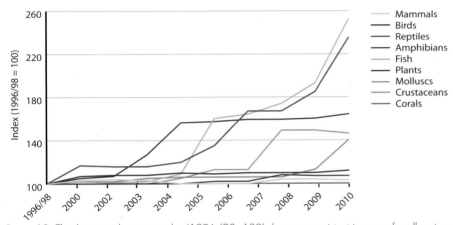

Figure 12: The threatened species index (1996/98=100) shows a consistent increase for all major groups of organisms studied between 1996 and 2010. Biodiversity loss continues to be of major concern, with species threatened at historically unprecedented rates. *Data source: GEO Data Portal, compiled from the International Union for Conservation of Nature (IUCN 2010)*

Ratio of area protected to maintain biological diversity to surface area

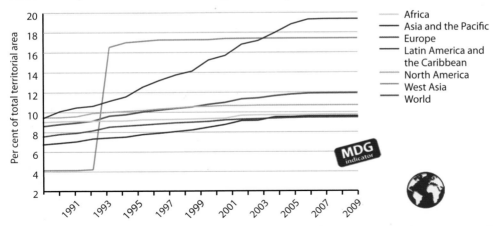

Figure 13: Ratio of area protected to maintain biological diversity to surface area, expressed as percentage of total territorial area, 1989-2009. Terrestrial and marine areas are combined. The extent of protected areas has increased during the past decade, particularly in Latin America and the Caribbean, where it doubled to almost one-fifth of the territorial area. Overall, about 12 per cent of the territorial area is currently protected. The Conference of the Parties to the Convention on Biological Diversity agreed in 2010 to a target of protecting 17 per cent of terrestrial and inland water areas, and 10 per cent of coastal and marine areas by 2020. *Data source: GEO Data Portal, compiled from UNEP-World Conservation Monitoring Centre (UNEP-WCMC 2010)*

Waste

A number of indicators have been developed for waste, but data availability is a major concern. Data on municipal waste collection are scarce, especially for developing countries (**Figure 14**).

Transboundary movements of hazardous waste are monitored, but insufficient data are available to show global or regional trends.

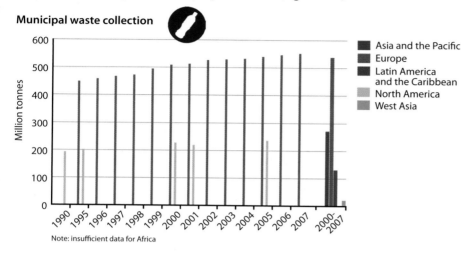

Municipal waste collection

Million tonnes

Asia and the Pacific
Europe
Latin America and the Caribbean
North America
West Asia

Note: insufficient data for Africa

Figure 14: Municipal waste collected in millions of tonnes, 1990-2007. The population served by private waste collectors or municipalities varies among regions. The limited data available at regional level suggests that the rate of municipal waste collection is highest in Europe and is steadily growing in that region, but information is very sparse and intermittent. Regional data alone hardly allow reliable conclusions to be drawn. *Data source: GEO Data Portal, compiled from UNSD/UNEP (2006), OECD/Eurostat (2008) and UNSD (2010)*

Water

The proportion of freshwater used for agriculture, industry and domestic purposes is monitored fairly well (**Figure 15**), but there are significant limitations to water quality monitoring in terms of regional or global use (**Figures 16** and **17**). Access to improved water supply and sanitation is probably one of the indicators for which reporting has been best carried out by individual countries (**Figure 18**). This indicator has important health as well as environmental relevance.

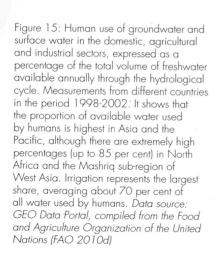

Figure 15: Human use of groundwater and surface water in the domestic, agricultural and industrial sectors, expressed as a percentage of the total volume of freshwater available annually through the hydrological cycle. Measurements from different countries in the period 1998-2002. It shows that the proportion of available water used by humans is highest in Asia and the Pacific, although there are extremely high percentages (up to 85 per cent) in North Africa and the Mashriq sub-region of West Asia. Irrigation represents the largest share, averaging about 70 per cent of all water used by humans. *Data source: GEO Data Portal, compiled from the Food and Agriculture Organization of the United Nations (FAO 2010d)*

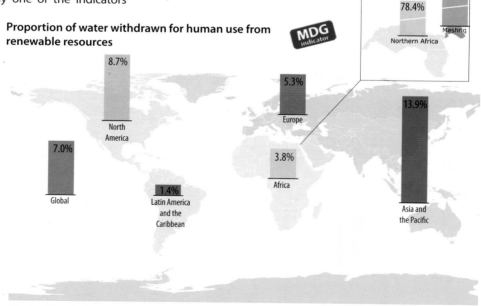

Proportion of water withdrawn for human use from renewable resources

MDG indicator

85.1% Mashriq
78.4% Northern Africa
8.7% North America
5.3% Europe
7.0% Global
1.4% Latin America and the Caribbean
3.8% Africa
13.9% Asia and the Pacific

Note: insufficient data for West Asia

Levels of dissolved oxygen in surface waters

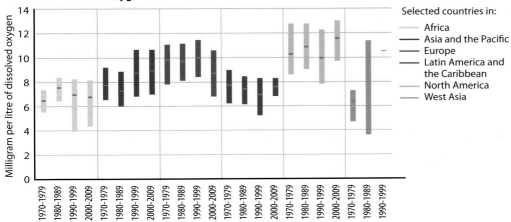

Figure 16: Levels of dissolved oxygen in surface waters expressed in milligrams per litre (mg/l) in selected countries, aggregated by regions. The data suggest that dissolved oxygen concentrations are generally within the widely accepted levels of 6 mg/l in warm water to 9.5 mg/l in cold water, as set, for example, in Australia (ANZECC 1992), Brazil (1986) and Canada (CCME 1999 and 2003). Data are supplied voluntarily by a wide range of contributors and are characterized by large statistical variations. They are not representative of all waters in these regions, or of each decade. *Data source: UNEP-GEMS/Water (2010)*

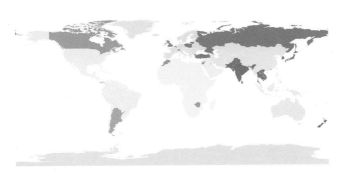

Figure 17: Countries in which dissolved oxygen measurement points were located for the water quality indicator in the period 2000-2009. The map shows the limited number of data points per region.

Proportion of population with sustainable acces to an improved water source and with access to improved sanitation

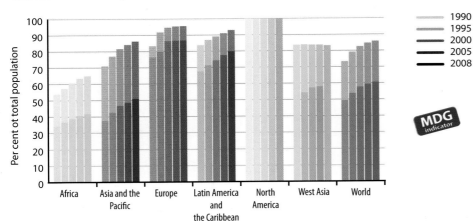

Figure 18: Improved drinking water (back) and improved sanitation coverage (front) as a percentage of the total population. While access to safe water supply continues to improve, challenges remain, notably in rural areas. Overall access to basic sanitation services also continues to improve in all parts of the world, although only about half the population of the developing world is using improved sanitation. *Data source: GEO Data Portal, compiled from WHO/UNICEF (2010)*

Environmental governance

Effective environmental governance is critical to respond in a timely fashion to emerging environmental challenges and address agreed environmental priorities. The number of signatories to environmental conventions is used as an indicator to track progress with regard to international environmental governance (**Figure 19**) (**Table 1**). However, this indicator also demonstrates the fragmentation of the environmental governance landscape. Looking more specifically at environmental management in companies and organizations, the number of voluntary ISO 14001 certifications is inceasing (**Figure 20**). The overall goal of this international standard is to minimize harmful effects on the environment and improve environmental performance.

Number of parties to multilateral environmental agreements

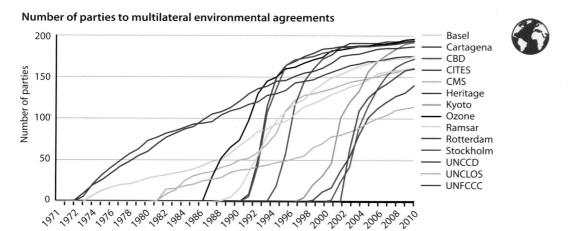

Figure 19: Number of parties to multilateral environmental agreements (MEAs), 1971-2010. These agreements comprise a major part of the international environmental governance system. The number of parties to the MEAs is the number of countries and political and/or economic integration organizations that have deposited instruments of ratification, accession, acceptance or approval for the 14 major MEAs shown here. The number of parties continues to increase, and many agreements are reaching the maximum number of countries. In all, the number of parties to these 14 MEAs has increased to 88 per cent of the maximum. *Data sources: GEO Data Portal, compiled from various MEA secretariats (see table below for details)*

Table 1: Number of parties to multilateral environmental agreements

Region (total number of countries)	Basel	Cartagena	CBD	CITES	CMS	Heritage	Kyoto	Ozone	Ramsar	Rotterdam	Stockholm	UNCCD	UNCLOS	UNFCCC	Sum	Potential	Per cent
Africa (53)	49	48	53	52	41	52	53	53	47	40	51	53	45	53	690	742	93
Asia and the Pacific (45)	36	35	46	33	15	41	45	46	30	25	38	46	34	46	516	630	81.9
Europe (50)	49	43	49	48	42	49	49	51	47	39	43	49	44	49	651	686	94.9
Latin America and the Caribbean (34)	30	28	33	32	12	32	33	33	27	26	30	33	28	33	410	476	86.1
North America (2)	1		1	2		2	1	2	2	1	1	2	1	2	18	24	75
West Asia (12)	10	6	11	8	4	11	11	11	7	9	9	10	9	11	127	168	75.6
Global (196)	**175**	**160**	**193**	**175**	**114**	**187**	**192**	**196**	**160**	**140**	**172**	**193**	**161**	**194**	**2 412**	**2 730**	**88.4**

Data source: GEO Data Portal, compiled from the Basel Convention on the Control of Transboundary Movements of Hazardous Wastes and Their Disposal (Basel), Cartagena Protocol of Biosafety to the CBD, CBD, CMS, CITES, Convention Concerning the Protection of the World Cultural and Natural Heritage (World Heritage), Kyoto Protocol to the UNFCCC (Kyoto), Vienna Convention for the Protection of the Ozone Layer and its Montreal Protocol on Substances that Deplete the Ozone Layer (Ozone), Convention on Wetlands of International Importance Especially as Waterfowl Habitat (Ramsar), Rotterdam Convention on the Prior Informed Consent Procedure for Certain Hazardous Chemicals and Pesticides in International Trade (Rotterdam), Stockholm Convention on Persistent Organic Pollutants (Stockholm), UN Convention to Combat Desertification (UNCCD), UN Convention on the Law of the Sea (UNCLOS) and UNFCCC

Number of certifications of the ISO 14001 standard

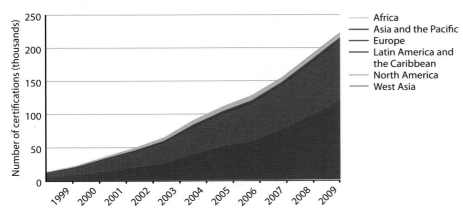

Figure 20: Number of ISO 14001 environmental management certifications, 1998-2009. This international standard is concerned with what companies and other organizations do to minimize the harmful effects of their activities on the environment and to achieve continual improvement in their environmental performance. The number of these certifications has grown considerably, particularly in Europe and Asia and the Pacific. The total number exceeded 200 000 in 2010. Although this increase can be seen as a positive development, certification only indicates the extent to which a company or organization conforms to its own stated environmental policy. *Data source: GEO Data Portal, compiled from the International Organization for Standardization (ISO 2010)*

Analyzing global and regional indicators

Considering all these indicators together—while bearing in mind that they represent an incomplete snapshot of the global environment—a mixed global picture emerges, with some promising signs of progress in areas such as renewable energy, forest certification, phasing out of ozone depleting substances, access to drinking water and ratification of environmental conventions. Huge challenges remain if trends are to be reversed in levels of greenhouse gas emissions, overexploitation of fish stocks and biodiversity loss. There is a need to address the underlying causes of environmental degradation.

Each indicator contributes a part of the story of ecosystem health and of efforts to work towards a green economy and an effective international environmental governance regime. Some research groups are working on concepts for combining the information provided through individual indicators into a single index (**Box 1**). Whereas trend analyses can be carried out for individual indicators or clusters of indicators, any forward-looking conclusion on overall environmental trends is constrained by the uncertainties and resilience associated with

natural systems and human behaviour, their interactions, and the lack of reliable, comprehensive and up-to-date data.

Constructing such a set of key indicators or composite indices is challenging, with overall data quality and availability still alarmingly poor and scarcely improving overall. Lack of good-quality data and consistent time-series for many environmental issues—such as water and air quality, waste collection and land degradation—severly hampers efforts to provide a sound basis for environmental decision-making, develop effective response strategies, and measure the impact of these strategies.

Policy makers are nevertheless continuously expected to take decisions related to the environment. Hence, it is critical to make available the most recent data on environmental pressures, state and trends. **Table 2** aims to do so by giving an overview of the latest data available for each of the key environmental indicators presented in this section. Where possible, data are presented at global and regional levels. Further information and technical notes are available from www.unep.org/yearbook/2011 and the GEO Data Portal (2010).

Table 2: Latest data for key environmental indicators

Indicator	Latest year on record	World	Africa	Asia and the Pacific	Europe	Latin America and the Caribbean	North America	West Asia	Unit of measurement
Carbon dioxide emissions	2007	29.5	1.1	12.9	6.5	1.6	6.4	0.97	billion tonnes of CO_2
Stratospheric ozone depletion	2009	38 656	2 651	30 249	-7 036	5 166	4 558	3 069	million tonnes ODP
Annual marine fish catch	2008	79.0	4.7	39.9	13.1	15.4	5.2	0.5	million tonnes
Forest harvest rate	2010	0.7	1.0	1.9	0.6	0.3	0.6		per cent
Forest coverage	2010	31.0	22.8	22.1	44.3	47.2	33.7	0.9	per cent of land area
Protected areas	2009	11.9	9.7	9.6	9.4	19.3	10.7	17.4	per cent of total territorial area
Forest certification	2010	136.9	7.4	6.2	60.2	13.5	49.6		million hectares
Water use	1998-2002	7.0	3.8	13.9	5.3	1.4	8.7		per cent
Access to safe water	2008	85.9	64.9	86.2	95.6	93.0	99.1	83.3	per cent of total population
Access to sanitation	2008	60.6	41.7	50.9	86.7	79.9	100.0		per cent of total population
ISO14001 certification	2009	223 149	1 536	119 480	89 745	4 793	6 446	1 149	number of certifications

Renewable energy	Latest year on record	Total all renewables (including waste)	Solar photovoltaics	Solar thermal	Wind	Hydro	Geothermal	Biofuels – total (liquid, solid, gas)	Biofuels – biogasoline and biodiesel	Tide, wave and ocean	
	2008	141.3	51 650.0	562.2	5 626.0	149.6	171.9	133.4	5 691.7	92.2	Index (1990=100)

Threatened species	Latest year on record	Mammals	Birds	Reptiles	Amphibians	Fishes	Plants	Molluscs	Crustaceans	Corals	
	2010	103.2	112.0	234.8	107.2	252.2	163.7	140.0	146.4	100.0	Index (1990=100)

Note: For certain indicators, no global or regional figures can be provided due to the local nature of the phenomenon or the lack of sufficient data. Examples include water quality, air pollution in cities and glacier change. The negative value for stratospheric ozone depletion in Europe is due to export, destruction or feedstock use of ozone depleting substances.

Box 1: Environmental indices

In addition to various environmental 'core sets of indicators' or 'dashboards', several attempts have been made to frame the global environment in a single index, usually combining multiple indicators or data sets. In the socio-economic domain, a well-known example is the Human Development Index, composed of data on income, education and life expectancy. In the environmental domain, examples include the Ecological Footprint, the Carbon Footprint, the Environmental Sustainability Index, the Environmental Performance Index, and Genuine (or Adjusted Net) Savings. These composite indices serve specific purposes and each has its advantages, disadvantages and limitations, as outlined, for example, in the report by Stiglitz and Fitoussi (2009), the 'Beyond GDP' initiative (Beyond GDP 2009) and the Global Project on 'Measuring the Progress of Societies'(OECD 2010). These initiatives point to limitations of using GDP as sole indicator of economic performance and social progress and call for a refinement by better capturing economic parameters including capital depreciation, standards of living and inequalities, as well as proper reflection of the environmental dimension and the concept of sustainability. It is also argued that quality-of-life is not only a material issue but also depends on non-economic factors such as health, environmental conditions, social relations and the like—and to be captured, all these require appropriate indicators (Stiglitz and Fitoussi 2009).

The Ecological Footprint looks at consumption and waste patterns and relates these to the surface area required to sustain them (Global Footprint Network 2010). According to the Ecological Footprint, humanity uses the equivalent of 1.5 planets to provide the resources we use and absorb the waste we produce. If current population and consumption trends continue, we will need the equivalent of two Earths to support mankind by the 2030s. Looking through the lens of the Ecological Footprint, a picture presents itself of people depleting the Earth and living off natural capital rather than choosing compromise for longer-term sustainability.

The Environmental Policy Index takes a more policy-oriented perspective (EPI 2010). It looks at countries' performance in terms of reaching established environmental policy goals. One can generally distinguish between industrialized and developing countries, in that major issues are derived from the resource and pollution impacts of industrialization (including greenhouse gas emissions and levels of waste) in developed countries and from lack of access to basic services, related to poverty and under-investment in basic environmental amenities, in developing countries.

References

ANZECC (1992) Australian Water Quality Guidelines for Fresh and Marine Waters, National Water Quality Management Strategy, Australian and New Zealand Environment and Conservation Council, Canberra, Australia

Beyond GDP (2009). Communication from the Commission to the Council and the European Parliament - GDP and beyond: measuring progress in a changing world. http://www.beyond-gdp.eu/

Boden, T.A., Marland, G. and Andres, R.J. (2010). Global, Regional, and National Fossil-Fuel CO_2 Emissions. Carbon Dioxide Information Analysis Center, Oak Ridge National Laboratory, U.S. Department of Energy, Oak Ridge, Tenn., U.S.A. http://cdiac.ornl.gov/trends/emis/tre_coun.html

Brazil (1986). Brazilian Surface Water Quality Guidelines. Resoluçao Conma No 20., de 18 de junho de 1986

Butchart, S. H. M., Stuart, H. M., Walpole, M., Collen, B., van Strien, A. et al.(2010). Global Biodiversity: Indicators of Recent Declines. Science, 328 (5982),1164-1168

CCME (Canadian Council of Ministers of the Environment) (1999). Canadian environmental quality guidelines for the Protection of Aquatic Life – Dissolved Oxygen (Freshwater), Winnipeg, Canada

CCME (Canadian Council of Ministers of the Environment) (2003). Canadian environmental quality guidelines for the Protection of Aquatic Life – Nitrate Ion, Winnipeg, Canada

EEA (2005). EEA core set of indicators – Guide. Technical report No. 1/2005. European Environment Agency, Copenhagen, Denmark

EPI (2010). Environmental Performance Index. Yale Center for Environmental Law and Policy, Yale University and Center for International Earth Science Information Network, and Columbia University. http://epi.yale.edu/

European Commission (2011), EUROSTAT, environment statistics database. http://epp.eurostat.ec.europa.eu/portal/page/portal/environment/data/main_tables

FAO (2005). Global Forest Resources Assessment 2005 (FRA) 2005. Key findings, Food and Agriculture Organization, Rome. http://www.fao.org/forestry/fra/fra2005/en/

FAO (2010a). Fisheries and Aquaculture Department: Global Statistical Collections. Food and Agriculture Organization, Rome. http://www.fao.org/fishery/statistics/en

FAO (2010b). Global Forest Resources Assessment 2010 (FRA) 2010. Key findings. Food and Agriculture Organization, Rome. http://www.fao.org/forestry/fra/fra2010/en/

FAO (2010c). FAOStat database. Food and Agriculture Organization, Rome. http://faostat.fao.org

FAO (2010d). AQUASTAT: FAO's Information System on Water and Agriculture. Food and Agriculture Organization, Rome. http://www.fao.org/nr/water/aquastat/main/index.stm

FSC (2010) Global FSC certificates. Forest Stewardship Council. http://www.fsc.org/facts-figures.html

GEO Data Portal (2010). United Nations Environment Programme. http://geodata.grid.unep.ch

Global Footprint Network (2010). http://www.footprintnetwork.org

GWEC (2011). Global wind capacity increases by 22% in 2010 - Asia leads growth. Global Wind Energy Council. http://www.gwec.net

IEA (2010). Renewable Information (2010 edition). International Energy Agency, Paris. http://data.iea.org/ieastore/product.asp?dept_id=101&pf_id=309

ISO (2010). The ISO Survey of Certifications 2009. International Organisation for Standardization, Geneva. http://www.iso.org/iso/iso_catalogue/management_standards/certification/the_iso_survey.htm

IUCN (2010). The IUCN Red List of Threatened Species (version 2010.4). International Union for Conservation of Nature. http://www.iucnredlist.org/about/summary-statistics

NOAA (2010). Science: The Antarctic Ozone Hole. http://www.ozonelayer.noaa.gov/science/ozhole.htm

OECD (2010). The Global Project on "Measuring the Progress of Societies". Organisation for Economic Co-operation and Development . http://www.oecd.org/pages/0,3417,en_40033426_40033828_1_1_1_1_1,00.html

OECD/Eurostat (2008). Questionnaire on the State of the Environment, Waste section Organisation for Economic Co-operation and Development, Paris. http://ec.europa.eu/eurostat/ramon/statmanuals/files/

Pandey K.D., Deichmann U., Wheeler D.R. and Hamilton, K.E. (2006). Ambient Particulate Matter Concentration in Residential and Pollution Hotspot Areas of World Cities: New Estimates Based on the Global Model of Ambient Particulates (GMAPS). The World Bank Development Economics Research Group and the Environment Department Working Paper. Washington D.C. http://go.worldbank.org/3RDFO7T6M0

SCBD (Secretariat of the Convention on Biological Diversity) (2010). Global Biodiversity Outlook 3. Montréal

Stiglitz, J. and Fitoussi, J.P. (2009). Measurement of Economic Performance and Social Progress. www.stiglitz-http://www.stiglitz-sen-fitoussi.fr/documents/rapport_anglais.pdf

UNEP-GEMS/Water (2010). GEMStat. United Nations Global Environment Monitoring System Water Programme. http://www.gemstat.org/default.aspx

UNSD (2010). Environmental indicators: Waste. United Nations Statistics Division, New York. http://unstats.un.org/unsd/environment/municipalwaste.htm

UNSD/UNEP (2006). Questionnaires on Environment Statistics, Waste section. United Nations Statistics Division, New York. http://unstats.un.org/unsd/environment/questionnaire2006.htm

UNEP (2010). Production and Consumption of Ozone Depleting Substances under the Montreal Protocol. United Nations Environment Programme, Ozone Secretariat, Nairobi. http://ozone.unep.org/Data_Reporting/Data_Access/

UNEP-WCMC (2010). World Database on Protected Areas. UNEP World Conservation Monitoring Centre, Cambridge. http://www.wdpa.org/Statistics.aspx

WGMS (2010). Glacier mass balance data 1980-2009, World Glacier Monitoring Service, Zurich. http://www.wgms.ch

WHO/UNICEF (2010). Joint Monitoring Programme (JMP) for Water Supply and Sanitation. World Heath Organization/The United Nations Children's Fund. http://www.wssinfo.org/data-estimates/introduction

World Bank (2006, 2008, 2010). World Development Indicators. The World Bank. http://data.worldbank.org/indicator

Acknowledgements

Events and Developments

Authors:
Susanne Bech and **Tessa Goverse**, United Nations Environment Programme, Nairobi, Kenya

Contributors:
Denis Couvet, National d'Histoire Naturelle, Paris, France
Johan Kuylenstierna, Stockholm Environment Institute – University of York, York, United Kingdom
Randall Martin, Dalhousie University, Halifax, Canada
Drew Shindell, Goddard Institute for Space Studies, National Aeronautics and Space Administration, New York, United States
Aaron van Donkelaar, Dalhousie University, Halifax, Canada

Reviewers:
Joseph Alcamo, United Nations Environment Programme, Nairobi, Kenya
Wang Delin, Forest Bureau of Ningxia Region, Yinchuan, China
Volodymyr Demkine, United Nations Environment Programme, Nairobi, Kenya
Jason Jabbour, United Nations Environment Programme, Nairobi, Kenya
Shi Jianning, Ningxia Technical College of Prevention and Control of Desertification, Yinchuan, China
Frédéric Jiguet, National d'Histoire Naturelle, Paris, France
Romain Julliard, National d'Histoire Naturelle, Paris, France
Mark Radka, United Nations Environment Programme, Paris, France
Frank Raes, Climate Change Unit European Commission - Joint Research Center, Varese, Italy
Veerabhadran Ramanathan, Scripps Institution of Oceanography, San Diego, United States
Jon Samseth, SINTEF, Trondheim, Norway
Anna Stabrawa, United Nations Environment Programme, Bangkok, Thailand
Anne Teyssèdre, National d'Histoire Naturelle, Paris, France
Zhijia Wang, United Nations Environment Programme, Nairobi, Kenya
Clarice Wilson, United Nations Environment Programme, Nairobi, Kenya
Yang Youlin, United Nations Economic and Social Commission for Asia and the Pacific, Bangkok, Thailand
Kaveh Zahedi, United Nations Environment Programme, Paris, France

Plastic Debris in the Ocean

Authors:
Sangjin Lee, Northwest Pacific Action Plan of UNEP, Busan, Republic of Korea
Katsuhiko Saido, Nihon University, Funabashishi, Japan
Jon Samseth, SINTEF, Trondheim, Norway
Douglas Woodring, Project Kaisei, Midlevels, Hong Kong

Science writer:
John Smith, Taunton, United Kingdom

Reviewers:
Jacqueline Alder, United Nations Environment Programme, Nairobi, Kenya
Ali Beba, Hong Kong University of Science and Technology, Kawloon, Hong Kong
Robert Bechtloff, Secretariat of the Stockholm Convention on Persistent Organic Pollutants, Geneva, Switzerland
Keith Christman, American Chemistry Council, Washington, D.C., United States
Christopher Corbin, Caribbean Regional Co-ordinating Unit, Kingston, Jamaica
Anna Cummins, The 5 Gyers Institute, Santa Monica, United States

Salif Diop, United Nations Environment Programme, Nairobi, Kenya
Marcus Eriksen, The 5 Gyers Institute, Santa Monica, United States
Heidi Fiedler, United Nations Environment Programme, Geneva, Switzerland
William R. Francis, Algalita Marine Research Foundation, Long Beach, United States
Francois Galgani, Centre de mediterranée, Zone de Bregaillon, Institut français de recherche pour l'exploitation de la mer, Cedex, France
Edward Kleverlaan, International Maritime Organization, London, United Kingdom
Thang Le Dai, Ministry of Natural Resources and Environment, Hanoi, Vietnam
Christa Licher, Ministry of Housing, Spatial Planning and the Environment, The Hague, the Netherlands
Rainer Lohmann, University of Rhode Island, New York, United States
David Osborn, United Nations Environment Programme, Nairobi, Kenya
Seba Sheavly, Sheavly Consultants, Virginia Beach, United States
Pak Sokharavuth, Ministry of Environment, Phnom Penh, Cambodia
Michael Stanley-Jones, Secretariat of the Stockholm Convention on Persistent Organic Pollutants, Geneva, Switzerland
Hideshige Takada, Tokyo University of Agriculture and Technology, Tokyo, Japan
Serguei Tarassenko, United Nations Office of Legal Affairs/Division for Ocean Affairs and the Law of the Sea, United Nations, New York, United States
Patrick ten Brink, Institute for European Environmental Policy, Brussels, Belgium
Martin Thiel, Universidad Católica del Norte, Coquimbo, Chile
Jorge Luis Valdes, Intergovernmental Oceanographic Commission, United Nations Educational, Scientific and Cultural Organization, Paris, France
Meryl J. Williams, Scientific and Technical Advisory Panel of the Global Environment Facility, Brisbane, Australia
Ron Witt, United Nations Environment Programme, Geneva, Switzerland
Christine Wellington-Moore, United Nations Environment Programme, Washington, D.C., United States

Phosphorus and Food Production

Authors:
Mateete Bekunda, Kampala International University (Nairobi Centre), Nairobi, Kenya
Dana Cordell, Institute for Sustainable Futures, University of Technology, Sydney, Australia
Jessica Corman, School of Life Sciences, Arizona State University, Tempe, United States
Arno Rosemarin, Stockholm Environment Institute, Stockholm, Sweden
Ignacio Salcedo, Federal University of Pernambuco, Brasilia, Brazil
Keith Syers, Naresuan University, Phitsanulok, Thailand

Science writer:
Tim Lougheed, Ottawa, Canada

Reviewers:
Jasper M. Dalhuisen, Ministry of Agriculture, Nature and Food Quality, The Hague, the Netherlands
Anjan Datta, United Nations Environment Programme, Nairobi, Kenya
Susan Etienne Greenwood, Scientific Committee on Problems of the Environment, Paris, France
R. Norberto Fernandez, United Nations Environment Programme, Nairobi, Kenya
John Freney, Commonwealth Scientific and Industrial Research Organization, Canberra, Australia
Cynthia Grant, Agriculture and Agri-Food Canada-Brandon Research Centre, Brandon, Canada
Julian Hilton, AleffGroup, London, United Kingdom
John Ingram, Global Environmental Change and Food Systems, University Centre for the Environment, Oxford, United Kingdom

Luc Maene, International Fertilizer Industry Association, Paris, France

Rob Mikkelsen, International Plant Nutrition Institute, Norcross, United States

Philip Moody, Department of Environment and Resource Management, Queensland Government, Brisbane, Australia

Malika Moussaid, AleffGroup, London, United Kingdom

Freddy Nachtergaele, Food and Agriculture Organization of the United Nations, Rome, Italy

Takehiro Nakamura, United Nations Environment Programme, Nairobi, Kenya

Véronique Plocq-Fichelet, Scientific Committee on Problems of the Environment, Paris, France

Terry L. Roberts, International Plant Nutrition Institute, Norcross, United States

Amit Roy, International Fertilizer Development Centre, Muscle Shoals, United States

Kaj Sanders, Ministry of Spatial Planning, Housing and Environment, The Hague, the Netherlands

Mary Scholes, University of Witwatersrand, Johannesburg, South Africa

Jaap Schröder, Wageningen University and Research Centre, Wageningen, the Netherlands

Stephen Twomlow, United Nations Environment Programme, Nairobi, Kenya

Holm Tiessen, Inter-American Institute for Global Change Research, São Paulo, Brazil

Massimiliano Zandomeneghi, United Nations Environment Programme, Nairobi, Kenya

 ## Emerging Perspectives on Forest Biodiversity

Authors:

Nick Brown, Department of Plant Sciences, University of Oxford, Oxford, United Kingdom

Richard Fleming, Canadian Forest Service, Natural Resources Canada, Great Lakes Forest Research Centre, Ontario, Canada

Jan Jenik, Department of Botany, Faculty of Science, Charles University, Prague, Czech Republic

Paula Kahumbu, Wildlife Direct, Nairobi, Kenya

Peter Kanowski, Australian National University, Canberra, Australia

Jan Plesnik, Agency for Nature Conservation and Landscape Protection of the Czech Republic, Prague, Czech Republic

Science writer:

Tahia Devisscher, Stockholm Environment Institute, Oxford, United Kingdom

Reviewers:

Steven Bernstein, International Union of Forestry Research Organizations, Ontario, Canada

Christophe Bouvier, United Nations Environment Programme, Geneva, Switzerland

Steven Cork, Australian National University and EcoInsights, Canberra, Australia

Robert Höft, Secretariat of the Convention on Biological Diversity, Montreal, Canada

Dirk Hölscher, Georg-August-Universität Göttingen, Göttingen, Germany

Mart Külvik, Estonian University of Life Sciences, Tartu, Estonia

Carolyn Tyhra Kumasi, Kwame Nkrumah University of Science and Technology, Kumasi, Ghana

Thomas E. Lovejoy, Heinz Center for Science, Economics and the Environment, Washington, D.C., United States

Brendan Mackey, Australian National University, Canberra, Australia

Vinod B. Mathur, Wildlife Institute of India, New Delhi, India

Mary Menton, Center for International Forestry Research, Lima, Peru

Christian Messier, Centre d'Étude de la Forêt, Quebec, Canada

Kieran Noonan-Mooney, Secretariat of the Convention on Biological Diversity, Montreal, Canada

Carolina Laura Morales, Instituto de Investigaciones en Biodiversidad y Medio Ambiente, Rio Negro, Argentina

Alex Mosseler, Canadian Forest Service, Atlantic Forestry Centre, Fredericton, Canada

Mary Njenga, World Agroforestry Centre, Nairobi, Kenya

Sarah A. Ogalleh, Centre for Training and Integrated Research in Arid and Semi-Arid Lands Development, Nanyuki, Kenya

John Parrotta, United States Forest Service, Research & Development, Arlington, United States

Ravi Prahbu, United Nations Environment Programme, Nairobi, Kenya

Ignacio Salcedo, Federal University of Pernambuco, Brasilia, Brazil

Nophea Sasaki, University of Hyogo, Hyogo, Japan

Jeffrey Sayer, Centre International Forestry Research, Bogor, Indonesia

Jörn Scharlemann, United Nations Environment Programme-World Conservation Monitoring Centre, Cambridge, United Kingdom

Johannes Stahl, Secretariat of the Convention on Biological Diversity, Montreal, Canada

Stephen Twomlow, United Nations Environment Programme, Nairobi, Kenya

Jerome Vanclay, Southern Cross University, Lismore, Australia

Mette Løyche Wilkie, Food and Agriculture Organization of the United Nations, Rome, Italy

 ## Key Environmental Indicators

Authors:

Andrea de Bono, United Nations Environment Programme/GRID-Europe, Geneva, Switzerland

Tessa Goverse, United Nations Environment Programme, Nairobi, Kenya

Jaap van Woerden, United Nations Environment Programme/GRID-Europe, Geneva, Switzerland

Reviewers:

Volodymyr Demkine, United Nations Environment Programme, Nairobi, Kenya

Robert Höft, Secretariat of the Convention on Biological Diversity, Montreal, Canada

Kelly Hodgson, United Nations Environment Programme-Global Environment Monitoring System/Water Programme, Burlington, Canada

Richard Robaerts, United Nations Environment Programme-Global Environment Monitoring System/Water Programme, Burlington, Canada

Ashbindu Singh, United Nations Environment Programme, Washington, D.C., United States

Matt Walpole, United Nations Environment Programme-World Conservation Monitoring Centre, Cambridge, United Kingdom

Michael Zemp, World Glacier Monitoring Service, Zürich, Switzerland

UNEP YEAR BOOK 2011 PRODUCTION

Project coordination/editors:
Susanne Bech and **Tessa Goverse** (editor-in-chief),
United Nations Environment Programme, Nairobi, Kenya

Project support:
Harsha Dave, Peter Gilruth, Daniel Lukhoni, Elijah Munyao and
Nyokabi Mwangi, United Nations Environment Programme, Nairobi, Kenya

Copy editor:
John Smith, Taunton, United Kingdom

Review editor for emerging issues:
Paul G. Risser, University of Oklahoma, Norman, United States

Graphics and images:
Márton Bálint, Budapest, Hungary, **Audrey Ringler** (cover design),
United Nations Environment Programme, Nairobi, Kenya

Special contributor:
Nick Nuttall, United Nations Environment Programme, Nairobi, Kenya

Collaborating partners on emerging issues:
Véronique Plocq-Fichelet and **Susan Etienne Greenwood**,
Scientific Committee on Problems of the Environment, Paris, France

Acronyms

APEC	Asia-Pacific Economic Cooperation
AQG	Air Quality Guideline
BC	black carbon
BPA	bisphenol A
CBD	Convention on Biological Diversity
CDIAC	Carbon Dioxide Information Analysis Center
CH_4	methane
CITES	Convention of International Trade in Endangered Species of Wild Fauna and Flora
COBSEA	Coordinating Body on the Seas of East Asia
CMS	Convention on Migratory Species of Wild Animals
CO_2	carbon dioxide
DDT	dichloro-diphenyl-trichloroethane
EcoQO	Ecological Quality Objective
EPI	Environmental Policy Index
EU	European Union
FAO	Food and Agriculture Organization of the United Nations
FSC	Forest Stewardship Council
GDP	Gross Domestic Product
GEF	Global Environment Facility
GEMS	Global Environment Monitoring System
GEO	Global Environment Outlook
GESAMP	Joint Group of Experts on the Scientific Aspects of Marine Environmental Protection
GHG	greenhouse gas
GIS	Geographic Information Systems
GLOBIO	Global Methodology for Mapping Human Impacts on the Biosphere
GPA	Global Programme of Action for the Protection of the Marine Environment from Land-based Activities
Gt	gigatonne
GW	gigawatt
HCFCs	hydrochlorofluorocarbons
HELCOM	Helsinki Commission
HELMEPA	Hellenic Marine Environment Protection Association
HFC	hydrofluorocarbon
HCH	hexachlorocyclohexane
ICT	information and communications technology
IEA	International Energy Agency
IFDC	International Fertilizer Development Center
IMAGE	Integrated modelling of global environmental change
IMDC	International Marine Debris Conference
IMO	International Maritime Organization
INTERMEPA	International Marine Environment Protection Association
IPBES	Intergovernmental Platform on Biodiversity and Ecosystem Services
IMAGE	Integrated modelling of global environmental change
IOC	Intergovernmental Oceanographic Commission
ISO	International Organization for Standardization
IUCN	International Union for Conservation of Nature
KIMO	Kommunenes Internasjonale Miljøorganisasjon (Local Authorities International Environmental Organisation)

MARPOL	International Convention for the Prevention of Pollution from Ships
MDG	Millennium Development Goal
MEA	multilateral environmental agreement
MEPA	Marine Environment Protection Association
Mt	megatonne
NCSA	National Capacity Self-Assessments
NGO	Non-governmental Organization
NOAA	National Oceanic and Atmospheric Administration
NO_2	nitrogen dioxide
NPK	nitrogen, phosphorus and potassium
ODA	Official Development Assistance
ODS	ozone depleting substances
ODP	Ozone Depletion Potential
OECD	Organisation for Economic Co-operation and Development
OSPAR	Convention for the Protection of the Marine Environment of the North-East Atlantic
O_3	ozone
PA	polyamide
PAHs	polyaromatic hydrocarbons
PBTs	persistent bio-accumulating and toxic substances
PCB	polychlorinated biphenol
PE	polyethylene
PEFC	Programme for Endorsement of Forest Certification schemes
PET	polyethylene terephthalate
PIC	Prior Informed Consent
PM	particulate matter
POPs	Persistent Organic Pollutants
PP	polypropylene
PS	polystyrene
PVC	polyvinyl chloride
REDD	Reducing Emissions from Deforestation and Forest Degradation in Developing Countries
RSP	Regional Seas Programme
SIDS	Small Island Developing States
SLCF	short-lived climate forcer
SO_2	sulphur dioxide
UNCCD	United Nations Convention to Combat Desertification
UNCLOS	United Nations Convention on the Law of the Sea
UNEP	United Nations Environment Programme
UNESCO	United Nations Educational, Scientific, and Cultural Organization
UNFCCC	United Nations Framework Convention on Climate Change
UNICEF	United Nations Children's Fund
UNIDO	United Nations Industrial Development Organization
UNSD	United Nations Statistics Division
USGS	United States Geological Survey
UV	ultraviolet
WDI	World Development Indicators
WHO	World Health Organization
WMO	World Meteorological Organization

Index

A

access and benefit sharing   3, 12, 13
adaptive management   52, 53, 57
agricultural productivity   16, 36, 39
agriculture   8, 16, 17, 29, 35, 40, 43, 48, 49, 68
agroforestry   16, 51
air pollution   7, 9, 10, 11, 63
air quality   6, 7, 8, 9, 10
algal bloom   12, 40
alien species   13, 25
Arctic   8, 21
assessment   7, 23, 30, 44, 61
aquaculture   21, 25
autoimmune diseases   9

B

behavioural changes   22, 28, 32, 44
benefits   7, 8, 21, 41, 47, 51, 53, 54, 56, 57
bioaccumulation   21, 26
biodegradable   26, 29, 33
biodiversity conservation   13, 14, 17, 47, 48,
    51, 52, 53, 54, 56, 57
biodiversity loss   1, 12, 47, 48, 49, 51, 61, 67
biodiversity monitoring   14, 15, 53, 67
biofuel   7, 12, 16, 39, 64, 72
biogas   43, 64, 72
biomagnification   27
biomass   8, 48, 55
black carbon   6, 7, 8, 9, 62, 64
buildings   4, 5

C

carbon budget   51
carbon dioxide emissions   51, 61, 63, 72
carbon stock   47, 51, 54
carcinogenicity   21, 28
certification   56, 57, 66, 71, 72
chemical contamination   13, 25-28
citizens   12, 15
citizen science   14, 15, 31, 67
cleanup costs   28, 31
climate change   1, 3-7, 8, 9, 12, 13, 16, 19, 48,
    51, 53-57
climate change adaptation   5, 12, 16, 51
climate change mitigation   5, 16, 47, 51, 53, 54

climate negotiations   1, 3, 7, 62
co-benefits   7, 43, 54
community   30, 47, 53, 57
concessions   54, 56
conservation   47, 48, 52, 53, 54, 56, 57
conservation agriculture   17
consumer awareness   32
consumer plastic   21, 22, 25
consumption   22, 35, 39, 40, 44, 48, 73
contour ploughing   42
convergence zone   21, 22, 23
costs   4, 12, 14, 22, 24, 28, 37, 40, 42, 43, 54
crop yield   7, 8, 9, 16, 17, 40

D

deforestation   5, 13, 47, 48, 53, 54, 56
degradation time   26
degraded ecosystems   52
deposits   37, 38
desertification   1, 16, 17, 19
developing countries   22, 39, 41, 47, 48, 53, 54
diet   16, 39, 44
disasters   1, 15
disease   9, 16, 48, 51
drinking water   22, 69, 71
drivers   22, 48, 56
drylands   17

E

ecological threshold   40, 51
ecological footprint   73
Ecological Quality Objective   24
ecological sanitation   43
economic growth   4, 47, 54
economic instruments   28, 32
ecosystem-based management   51, 57
ecosystem health   28, 71
ecosystem services   52, 54, 56
eco-tourism   54
education   28, 29, 30, 32, 42
electricity generation   3, 4, 5
emission gap   5, 6
endocrine disruption   21, 26, 28
endocrine system   26
energy   1-5, 22, 31, 32, 37, 43, 48, 64
energy efficiency   3, 4

energy generation   22, 32, 43, 48
energy security   4
environmental benefits   40
environmental conventions   1, 2, 3, 12, 19,
    47, 70
environmental governance   3, 56, 70, 71
environmental impact   24, 35, 41
environmental management certifications   71
environmental pressure   25, 32, 35, 47, 48, 56,
    57, 71
environmental sustainability   1, 3, 61, 72
erosion   17, 35, 40, 41, 42, 44
eutrophication   35, 39, 40, 41, 42
excreta   35, 40, 41, 43
extended producer responsibility   32

F

farmers   35, 36, 37, 38, 41, 43, 44
farming practices   35
fertilizer   9, 35-44
fishing   14, 23, 25, 28, 31
fish stocks   39, 65, 71
fishing industry   2, 21, 28
fishing nets   25, 26, 29, 31
forest cover   47, 48, 66
food production   4, 7, 16, 35, 40, 44
food security   9, 12, 16, 37
food waste   21, 35, 40, 44
forest biodiversity   47-57
forest certification   56, 61, 66, 71, 72
forest area   47, 66, 72
forest degradation   5, 47, 48, 52, 53, 54, 56
forest ecosystems   47, 48, 51, 54, 56
forest fires   3, 7, 48, 51
forest governance   56, 57
forest management   47, 50, 51, 53, 54, 56, 57
forest remnants   51, 52, 57
fouling   21, 26, 28
fossil fuel   4, 7, 8, 9, 47, 63, 64
freshwater ecosystem   12, 26, 40
fulmar   24, 25

G

Geographic Information System   53
glacier   3, 64, 7
global food consumption   16, 28

response   27, 40, 51, 53, 54, 57
restoration   12, 14, 17, 17, 48, 52
roundwood   66
run-off   36, 37, 42

S

sanitation   1, 2, 43, 69, 72
scenario   5, 48, 49
seafloor sediments   37
secondary forests   51, 56, 57
sewage   21, 43
shifting sands   17
short-lived climate forcers   7, 8, 9
siltation   42
small island developing states   23, 32
soil erosion   35, 41, 42, 44
soil fertility   35
solar energy   3, 4, 64, 73
solution   13, 16, 29, 32, 44
soot   62
species   21, 24, 25, 40, 47, 48, 51, 52
stakeholders   44, 53, 54
Stockholm Convention   2, 18, 21, 26
stratospheric ozone   6, 62, 72
struvite   43
sulphur dioxide   11
surface water   12
sustainable agriculture   16, 17
sustainable development   1, 3, 4, 17, 19

sustainable forest management   47, 54, 56
sustainable land management   13, 17, 41

T

technological innovation   32, 40, 43
technology transfer   28, 54
terrestrial system   39
threatened species   55, 67, 72
threshold   40, 51
timber industries   50
timescales   52
topsoil   42
tourism   21, 23, 28, 30, 32, 54
toxic substances   21, 26, 27
transboundary movements   68
tree cover   14
tree species   51
trend analyses   71
tropical forests   56
tropospheric ozone   6-8
tuna   65

U

urban development   12
urban air pollution   10, 11, 63
urban area   11, 40, 43
urbanization   12, 14, 23, 37

V

volunteer   14, 15, 31
volunteer monitoring schemes   14

W

waste   21, 22, 23, 25, 28, 29, 30, 32, 35, 37, 39, 41, 43, 44, 68, 71, 72, 73
waste management   1, 4, 8, 21, 22, 28, 32, 37, 40, 43, 68
wastewater treatment   7, 8, 12, 36, 43
water column   23, 24, 26
water flow regulation   47, 52
water purification   12
water quality   39, 42, 69
water resources management   17
water supply   68, 69
water use   68, 72
wheat production   8, 9, 16

Z

zooplankton   23